The New
Guide to

GOOD
CHESS

By I. A. Horowitz

GOLDEN PRESS · NEW YORK

FOR
EDNA

Contents

PART I

WHAT THE GAME OF CHESS IS ALL ABOUT

PART IV
CHESS MOVIES

PART V
MODEL GAMES

Part I
What the Game of Chess Is All About

Chess is a game for two adversaries. It is played on a chessboard with 32 chessmen—16 White (or the lighter colored) for one player, 16 Black (or the darker colored) for the other. Each player moves in turn, White first.

Each player controls equal forces: eight Pawns and eight other pieces. For each the most important, though not the most powerful, is the King. While at any given turn to play there may be lesser objectives, the constant, primary, and ultimate goal of the game is to snare the hostile monarch in an operation called "checkmate."

Chess is a universal game. Its devotees exist in every nation on the globe. Its variations are infinite. But it is easy to learn and easy to understand in an elementary sense. After an hour of study, the tyro may begin playing—badly, indifferently, or even fairly well.

This book is planned to aid the absolute beginner to advance to the ranks of the experienced player. Everything needed for basic training is included.

However, the beginner should not proceed to the second lesson until he fully comprehends the first!

The first, ever to be retained, is, in the words of a chess enthusiast: "The King, the King! To checkmate the King!"

The Board

The chessboard is the battlefield. It is a large square, of any of various materials, "checkered" into 64 equal squares alternately light and dark colored. Any contrasting colors may do, but white and black are common and are the official designations.

Illustration 1

BLACK

WHITE

The board

The horizontal lines of squares, running from left to right, are called "ranks." Each rank is made up of eight squares: four white and four black. In all, there are eight ranks on the board.

The vertical lines of squares, running up and down the board, are called "files." The vertical files correspond in detail to the horizontal ranks.

Viewing the squares diagonally, the board also consists of "diagonals," each of one color—either all white or

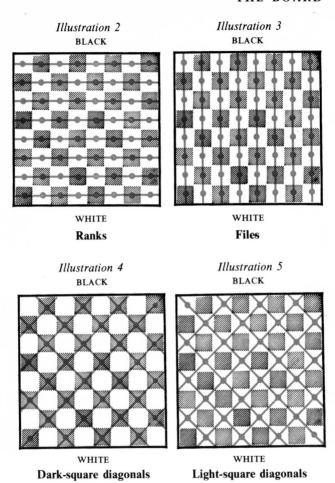

Illustration 2
BLACK

WHITE
Ranks

Illustration 3
BLACK

WHITE
Files

Illustration 4
BLACK

WHITE
Dark-square diagonals

Illustration 5
BLACK

WHITE
Light-square diagonals

all black. Unlike ranks and files, diagonals vary in their numbers of squares—from two to eight.

The board is always to be placed so that each player has a white square at his right-hand corner.

Illustration 6

white square

white square

Board and men in original setup

The Chessmen

Illustration 6 shows the board and the chessmen as they are arrayed at the start of a game. At this point, the near side, White, is to move. After he selects and makes his move, then Black takes his turn.

The eight chessmen in White's front rank are Pawns; behind them stand the "pieces" (a term which generally excludes pawns): From left to right, Rook (or Castle), Knight, Bishop, Queen, King, Bishop, Knight, and Rook.

Black's men, directly opposite in each instance, bear the same names.

The King is distinguished by its crown, most often a cross, sometimes an orb or orb plus cross. The Queen has an eight-spiked crown, symbol of its eight-directional move. The Rooks can be recognized as castles, the Bishops have bishop's mitres, and the Knights are represented as horse's heads. The pieces are subdivided as being initially on either the Queen's side of the board or the King's, and they retain these designations throughout the game: thus Queen Rook, abbreviated to QR, Queen Knight (QN), Queen Bishop (QB), Queen (Q), King (K), King Bishop (KB), King Knight (KN), and King Rook (KR). The phonetic N is used for Knight today, though older texts and some present-day ones employ the cumbersome Kt. (Kt takes more space and may be misread for K).

The Black men standing opposite have the same names; reading from *Black's* left to right: KR, KN, KB, K, Q, QB, QN, and QR, with Pawns before each piece.

The names of the Pawns, however, vary. They start initially with the names of the pieces before which they stand, but they change if they move to another file. Thus, the White Pawns in the photograph are, from left to right, the Queen Rook Pawn (QRP), Queen Knight Pawn (QNP), Queen Bishop Pawn (QBP), Queen Pawn (QP), King Pawn (KP), King Bishop Pawn (KBP), King Knight Pawn (KNP), and King Rook Pawn (KRP). However, as play progresses, they are renamed by the file on which they stand. Thus, if late in the game, the White Pawn initially known as the QRP moves one or more files to the right, it becomes a QNP or a QBP.

At the start of a game, the Kings and Queens are directly opposite each other. For convenience, it may be remembered that the Queens take their own colors: the White Queen starts on a white square, the Black Queen on a black square (White and Black in capital letters indicates the sides; in lower case, the squares).

Illustration 7

Diagram of men and board

Illustration 7 shows how chessmen are represented diagramatically in most textbooks. Note and learn to recognize each man and square "diagramatically."

Illustration 8 **The chessmen**

King   Queen   Bishop   Knight   Rook   Pawn

How the Men Move

Each of the six different kinds of pieces has its own distinctive powers of movement. The six kinds are described below.

The Rook. The Rook has, perhaps, the simplest move to describe. It travels in a straight line on a file or a rank.

The Rook can go forward or backward on a file, or to the right or left on a rank. It traverses any number of empty squares in one move. The extent of its move

Illustration 9

How the Rook moves

is limited only by the edges of the board or by obstructing men on the board.

Illustration 10

Limits of a Rook move

In illustration 10, the White Rook is severely limited. It cannot "jump" its own men; thus it cannot move to the left, as the White Knight blocks its way. It can move forward one or two squares, or backward one or two squares. As for the opposing Black men in its paths, it can move onto the square on which any one of them stands. By so doing it captures that man and the man is removed from the board. Thus, the White Rook can move backward three squares, capturing the Black Queen, which is then removed from the board.

Similarly, on Black's turn to play, the Black Rook can move either one square to the right (no further as it cannot go off the board), one square to the left, or one square down the board. It cannot go up the board as its own Bishop blocks it in that direction. However, it can capture either the White Knight or the White Pawn by moving two squares in the proper direction.

Note that on an open board, unobstructed by its own or opposing men, the Rook always commands seven squares along a rank and seven along a file. It does not command the square on which it stands.

The Bishop. The Bishop moves almost in another world from the Rook; it moves only along diagonals.

Illustration 11

How the Bishop moves

Otherwise, the Bishop has the same powers as a Rook. It can travel the full length of a diagonal, stopped only by the edge of the board or by the obstruction of a man on the diagonal. It cannot "jump" its own men; it can capture enemy men in just the ways described for the Rook.

Illustration 12

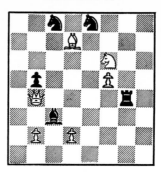

Limits of a Bishop move

In illustration 12, the White Bishop can "move" only to two squares: the ones diagonally down the board to its left or right. But it can capture either the Black Knight or the Black Pawn. In such a capture, the player places the Bishop on the square occupied by the enemy man and removes that man from the game. The Black Bishop (on Black's turn to move, of course) can move to either of two squares: the first or the second square diagonally upward to the right. Or it can capture the White Queen or either of the two White Pawns that are diagonally beneath it.

Note that on an entirely open board, the Bishops command a varying number of squares according to the lengths of the diagonals on which they stand. With all men removed from the diagram above except the two Bishops, the White Bishop would command a total of nine squares: five along its long diagonal; four along the other. (Like the Rook, the Bishop does not command the square on which it stands; and, in fact, no chessman does.) The Black Bishop would command a total of 11 squares: seven along the long diagonal; four along the other.

Note also that any Bishop remains on the same-colored squares throughout the game. Thus, the two Bishops in illustration 12 can never encounter each other (technically, they are known as "Bishops of opposite colors," meaning of opposite-colored squares). Thus, also, any one Bishop can affect only half the chessboard. Hence, its power is less than that of a Rook which can, in time, reach any square on the board.

The Queen. The Queen combines the powers of Rook and Bishop. It moves along ranks, files, and diagonals, but, like them, only in one direction per move.

Illustration 13

How the Queen moves

In short, on any one turn to move, the Queen can
travel in any one of eight directions: forward or back
vertically, or left or right horizontally, like the Rook;
or diagonally in any one of four directions, like the
Bishop. It cannot, however, veer in transit: it either
moves like a Rook or like a Bishop, not as a combination
of the two on any one move. Note, however, that, in
time, it can reach any square on the board—if need be
along a diagonal on one turn, then along rank or file
on the next turn.

Illustration 14

Limits of a Queen move

Like the Rook and Bishop, the Queen can move any
number of squares in any one direction at any one turn,
limited only by the edge of the board and by obstructing
men. In illustration 14, the Queen can move one or two
squares up or down the board or right or left (like a
Rook); or diagonally up one square to the right or left,
or diagonally down one or two squares to the right (like
a Bishop). Or it can capture any single one of the Black
men on the board. Like Rook and Bishop, the Queen
cannot jump over any men; and, if any one of the Black

men were White (like the Queen), the Queen simply could not move to the square on which that (White) man was standing.

Note that the Queen has the greatest range of any piece and is consequently the most powerful unit (aside from the opposing Queen, its equal) on the board.

The King. The regular King move is very simple. It can go one square in any direction: forward, backward, right, or left, or in any one of the four diagonal directions.

Illustration 15

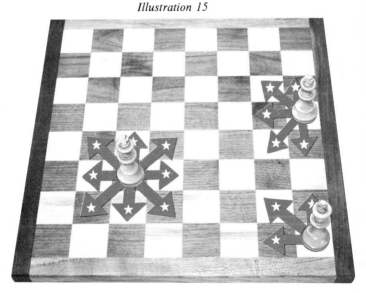

How the King moves

Note that on the edge of the board the King moves are limited. The King normally has a choice of one of eight moves; on an edge, one of five; in a corner, one of three.

But the King has other limitations, too. The King must be preserved or the game is lost. Hence, the King cannot move into the direct line of fire of an enemy man. Under the rules, such a move is illegal. Nor can the King be allowed to remain under fire of an enemy man, should the enemy man attack it. The attack on the King by an opposing piece is known as a "check," and the King, under the rules of the game, must avoid all checks. It cannot move into check; it must move out of check. However, if the King is checked and cannot escape from check by moving, by interposition of its own men, or by capture of the checking man, then the King is "checkmated," and the opposing side wins the game.

Illustration 16

Limits of a King move

In illustration 16, White's King is not under attack, "under check," and so the White King does not have to move. If White chooses to move his King, however, he has the following possible choices and limitations: the King cannot be moved directly forward as that path is blocked by its own Pawn, nor directly back as that route is cut off by its own Rook. If those squares were empty, the King still could not move into them as it would be moving into check by the enemy Bishop beside it. The King cannot be moved diagonally forward to the left as it would then be moving into check by the enemy Rook; for the same reason, the King cannot be moved horizontally to the left. The King *can* be moved diagonally forward to the right; and the King can capture the Black Rook, Bishop, or Knight.

On Black's turn to move, in the illustrative grouping at the top of the diagram, the King must be moved because it is under attack by the White Bishop. It cannot move to the squares occupied by its own men. Of the remaining squares within the range of the King, the King cannot capture the White Knight on the white square because it would then (still) be attacked by the White Bishop; it cannot capture the other Knight for, as will be seen when the Knight moves have been learned, the two Knights "protect" each other and the Black King would be moving into check by the White Knight on the white square; nor can it move to the black square to its left as that is within range of the White Knight on the white square. But the Black King does have a choice of two moves: it can move upward diagonally to the right, or it can capture the White Bishop.

The King has one other, special power or move, in combination with a Rook, which will be described later under "Castling" (page 34).

The Knight. The Knight has a peculiar move, a move which occurs only in chess, or in games derived from chess.

Illustration 17

How the Knight moves

The move can be and has been described in a number of ways. The beginner can take the description which seems to come most naturally to him.

The Knight move is always of the same length, and in the form of a capital "L" turned in any direction. The move can be made:

A) Two squares vertically; then one square horizontally.

B) Two squares horizontally; then one square vertically.

In effect, the Knight jumps over one rank, and lands on the next, in the file to its right or left, on a square of the opposite color from the one on which it started.

If the Knight were to make two successive moves in the same direction, its "line of travel" would lie between the lines of a Bishop and of a Rook.

Illustration 18

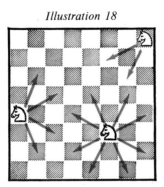

Some Knight moves diagramed

Illustration 18 shows that a Knight on or near the middle of the board can travel in any one of eight directions (lower right). On the side of the board, the Knight can travel in any one of four directions. And from a corner of the board (upper right), the Knight can make but one of two moves.

The Knight captures exactly as it moves. That is, to effect a capture, the Knight makes its peculiar, normal move, and, if it lands on a square occupied by an enemy man, that man is removed from the game, or "captured."

The Knight move is truly a "jump." Thus, the Knight, and only the Knight, can jump over intervening men—its own or the opponent's. It cannot, however, land on a square that is occupied by one of its own men.

Illustration 19

How the Knight captures

In illustration 19, the White Knight, on White's turn to move, can capture any one of the Black men. On Black's turn to move, if Black chooses to move his Knight, that Knight can capture either of the White Rooks or the White Bishop or the White Knight or the White Queen or the White Pawn within its range (the further White Pawn is out of its reach).

The Knight, in sum, has a limited move. It travels only the approximate distance of two squares (in the direction described), no more, no less. It is a short-stepping piece, though longer-stepping than the King; it has less range than Bishop, Rook, or Queen. But, unlike the Bishop, it can, in time, reach any square on the board. Also, since the Knight "jumps," it is the only piece which can move at the beginning of the game (Pawns can, but no other pieces), and it is useful in a board clogged with Pawns and pieces when the far-ranging Bishop, Rook, and Queen have difficulty in finding open lines of travel. Consequently, the Knight, despite its short step, ranks as a fighting unit almost but not quite as strong as a Bishop.

The Pawn. The lowly Pawn is in world-wide proverbs readily expendable as fuel for an attack, as bait for a lure, or just to open lines for the pieces which cannot jump over it. But it has other uses, too: shelter for the King, framework for a positional stronghold, and obstruction for enemy men. And, when it reaches the furthest rank, it can be promoted to any piece (except King) desired by its player, even a powerful Queen.

The basic Pawn move is one square forward. However, for its first move, and *only* the first for each Pawn, it can go two squares forward.

Illustration 20

How the Pawn moves: here the Pawn may move to either star

Note that the Pawn, unlike all other chessmen, can never retreat. Thus, whatever weaknesses a Pawn move leaves behind it cannot be repaired, and the "Pawn skeleton" (deployment of Pawns), has great effect on a player's strategic position in the game.

Also, the Pawn differs from other men in capturing by a distinctive move. It *moves* straight forward, but it *captures* diagonally, to right or left, forward. Thus, a Pawn commands the squares to the right and left just before it.

Illustration 21

How the Pawn captures

To sum up, a Pawn moves one square forward (except for the two-square option on its first move), but it captures by moving diagonally forward onto a square occupied by an enemy man (which is removed, as in all captures, from the board). It also can capture "en passant," a move to be described presently. In illustration 21, the White Pawn can capture the Black Knight; but not the Black Pawn, nor, of course, the White Knight.

Pawn Promotion. According to the rules of chess, when a Pawn reaches the eighth and final rank, it must be promoted to a piece of its own color—becoming a new Knight, new Bishop, new Rook, or new Queen. It cannot become a King nor can it remain a Pawn. Since the Queen is so powerful a piece, the Pawn is usually promoted to a Queen, and hence promotion in general is spoken of as "queening." For special reasons, usually ones which aid in effecting an early mate or at least afford a useful check, the Pawn may be made a lesser piece at the option of its player. But it *must* be promoted.

Illustration 22a	*Illustration 22b*

Pawn to be promoted	**The Pawn promoted**

Pawns are at their strongest when abreast, as each Pawn then has a ready defense. If one of the Pawns is attacked, its simple move forward leaves it protected by the adjacent Pawn(s). For, if an enemy man captures the lead Pawn, that man is subject to capture by the supporting Pawn on the next turn to move.

Illustration 23   *Illustration 24*

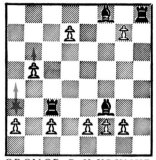

Various Pawn formations   Q R Q N Q B Q K K B K N K R
                                Various Pawn situations

Thus, in illustration 23, the pristine White Pawns on the left are fully ready to support one another. The doubled White Pawns on the right cannot protect or be protected by each other, and the forward one retards the hind one so it cannot move to escape capture if threatened by an enemy piece. The two Black Pawns on the right are weakened by the fact that one has moved and can no longer protect its colleague. Also, as an enemy piece can be lodged just in front of the rearmost Pawn without ever being attacked by a Black Pawn, Black's Pawn deployment is weak. Such a weakness is known as a "Pawn hole." The tripled Black Pawns on the left have, all three together, only the driving force of the foremost; none of the three can protect the others; and the two left behind, particularly, are sitting targets for attack by White pieces.

Here is a review of Pawn factors. In illustration 24, there are eight White Pawns. The leftmost is on its original square and so may move one or two squares

forward, at choice. The next on the Queen Knight file
(indicated by QN under the diagram) has advanced and
can now move but one square forward. The Pawn on
the QB file is blocked by Black's Rook (the Pawn captures diagonally forward and has no command over the
square immediately in front of it), so this Pawn simply
cannot move. The Pawn on the Q file has advanced to
the seventh rank: it can advance one rank further and
then must be promoted to a new piece—Queen, Rook,
Bishop, or Knight—of its own color. Since a new Queen
would add so much power to White's game, Black should
do his utmost to stop that Pawn. Here, if it is Black's
move, he can conveniently do so by capturing the advanced White Pawn on the KN file with his Bishop,
leaving his Rook free to defend the eighth rank, should
White, on his turn, try to promote his Q Pawn.

The Pawn on the K file can either move forward its
optional one or two squares or it can capture the Black
Bishop. In chess, it may be remarked here, captures are
optional, not mandatory. The Pawn on the KB file, like
that on the QB file, cannot move at all here.

The more forward of the doubled Pawns on the KN
file has three possible moves. It can move directly forward to be promoted (and immediately captured by
Black's Rook); it can capture Black's Bishop (and, again,
be promoted and then captured by Black's Rook); or it
can capture Black's Rook, be promoted, and be in no
danger of capture itself. The rearmost of these two
doubled Pawns can, like the Pawn on the K file, either
advance one or two squares or capture the Bishop.

Note, in relation to Pawn promotions, that the advance and the promotion are both done on one turn.

The move begins with the touching or grasping of the Pawn, continues with the advancing of it, and concludes with the removal of the Pawn and its replacement by the chosen piece on the eighth-rank square. Note also that the promotion takes place without regard to what pieces may still be on the board. When White promotes, he can make a new Queen even though he still has his original Queen, or a new Knight even though he has both his original Knights. (Because a chess set usually has but one Queen per side, in actual practice an inverted Rook is used for a second Queen—see illustration 25.) In short, it is theoretically possible for one side after queening an eighth Pawn to have as many as nine

Illustration 25

Queening

Queens on the board—the original Queen plus eight "promoted" Queens. Or he might have as many as ten Rooks, or ten Bishops, or ten Knights.

En Passant. There is a peculiar mode of Pawn capturing known as "en passant" (French for "in passing"). It involves a Pawn already established on its fifth rank and an attempt by the opponent to by-pass that Pawn with one of his own, making a two-square first move on an adjacent file.

Illustration 26 shows a position with the essential elements for an en passant capture. White's Pawn is on its fifth rank.

Illustration 26   *Illustration 27*

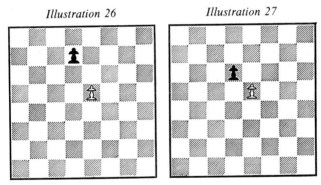

Pawns before   **Pawns after**
an "en passant"   **a one-square Black move**

In illustration 27, Black has advanced his Pawn one square. The optional two-square move was a late modification in the rules of chess. In the old days, the Black Pawn could not by-pass the White but, as here, had to make a move which could permit White on his next turn to capture with his own Pawn.

In illustration 28, Black has elected to make a two-square move. The important fact is that if Black's Pawn cannot be stopped, it might perhaps travel on to queen. As a new Queen would be so powerful, the game could be won thus.

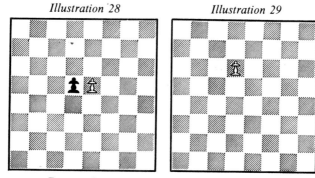

Illustration 28   *Illustration 29*

Pawns after   **After the**
a two-square Black move   **"en passant" capture**

By the en passant rule, however, the White Pawn can capture the passing Black Pawn just as though it had moved but one square. White has effected such a capture in illustration 29, moving his Pawn one square diagonally forward and removing the Black Pawn from the board.

Note that the position after White's en passant capture is just what it would have been if White elected to make a Pawn capture in the position shown in illustration 27. The White Pawn moves diagonally forward one square, and the Black Pawn is removed from the board, if White chooses to capture, whether the Black Pawn moves one or two squares forward.

In illustration 30, the case is similar, with colors

Illustration 30

A White Pawn tries to by-pass

reversed. The White Pawn has just moved two squares forward, by-passing a Black Pawn on its fifth rank. Black now has the right to capture en passant if he so chooses.

Capturing en passant is no more mandatory than any other capture. It is, however, a right which exists *only* for the next turn to play. If White has just moved his Pawn two squares, Black can now capture en passant. But if Black employs his next turn to play to make some other move, he cannot, on the succeeding turn or on any turn thereafter, make this particular en passant capture. Note also that if the White Pawn in illustration 30 had arrived on the fourth rank by a one-square move—that is, if the White Pawn was previously on the third rank and now had just moved to the fourth rank—no en passant capture would be possible.

To review: an en passant capture is possible only if the capturing Pawn stands on its fifth rank, if the by-passing Pawn has done so by moving two squares on an immediately adjacent file, and if the en passant capture is made on the very next move.

Castling. There is a special and unique movement of the pieces called "castling." It is made by the King and a Rook in combination, a dual action which is counted as a single move. It may be performed with either Rook, on the Kingside or on the Queenside.

In the process, the King moves two squares toward the Rook involved. Then the Rook is placed on the square horizontally next beyond the new position of the King. (See illustrations 31a, 31b, 32a, 32b.)

For castling to be legal, certain conditions are mandatory:

1. The squares between King and Rook must be vacant.

Illustration 31a

Kingside castling—White men

2. King and Rook must stand each on its original square with neither yet having been moved.

3. The King must not be in check when castling.

4. The King must not cross over squares "under check."

5. The King must not move on to a square "under check."

If these conditions all obtain, castling is permissible. They may obtain several, even many times during a game; but, by definition, once a side has castled, it can never do so again.

In executing the move of castling, one precaution is necessary. Under the rules of play, a man touched must

Illustration 31b

Queenside castling—White men

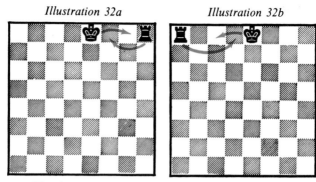

Illustration 32a   *Illustration 32b*

Kingside castling—   **Queenside castling—**
Black men   **Black men**

be moved; if several are touched, the opponent can choose which is to be moved. So, in castling, King and Rook should be moved simultaneously, or the King first (since his two-square move can be only for castling, the opponent cannot claim it is only a simple King move). Otherwise, the opponent may insist on a penalty: that just the King or just the Rook (not both as intended in castling) be moved.

Note also that a "promoted Rook" (one made from a Pawn which has reached the eighth rank) cannot take part in castling.

Chess Notation

Reading, writing, and 'rithmetic, the three R's of childhood, facilitate the processes of perception. And in chess, too, reading and writing are quite possible.

To be able to record or to understand the record of an actual game, it is necessary first to know the abbreviated names of each square on the chessboard. Then a movement of a man from one square to another can be described and followed.

Notation of the Chessboard. On the accompanying chart are the abbreviated names of each square. Names because there are two, one from the point of view of White's side; one from Black's.

Illustration 33

BLACK

QR1 QR8	QN1 QN8	QB1 QB8	Q1 Q8	K1 K8	KB1 KB8	KN1 KN8	KR1 KR8
QR2 QR7	QN2 QN7	QB2 QB7	Q2 Q7	K2 K7	KB2 KB7	KN2 KN7	KR2 KR7
QR3 QR6	QN3 QN6	QB3 QB6	Q3 Q6	K3 K6	KB3 KB6	KN3 KN6	KR3 KR6
QR4 QR5	QN4 QN5	QB4 QB5	Q4 Q5	K4 K5	KB4 KB5	KN4 KN5	KR4 KR5
QR5 QR4	QN5 QN4	QB5 QB4	Q5 Q4	K5 K4	KB5 KB4	KN5 KN4	KR5 KR4
QR6 QR3	QN6 QN3	QB6 QB3	Q6 Q3	K6 K3	KB6 KB3	KN6 KN3	KR6 KR3
QR7 QR2	QN7 QN2	QB7 QB2	Q7 Q2	K7 K2	KB7 KB2	KN7 KN2	KR7 KR2
QR8 QR1	QN8 QN1	QB8 QB1	Q8 Q1	K8 K1	KB8 KB1	KN8 KN1	KR8 KR1

WHITE

The files are designated from the pieces which are posted on them at the start of a game (just, in fact, as described on page 11). From White's left, therefore, the files read: QR (Queen Rook), QN, QB, Q, K, KB, KN, and KR. And the Black reading of the files, from right to left this time, is exactly the same.

In speaking of the board, also, it is customary to refer to the Kingside (that on which K, KB, KN, and KR originally stood) and the Queenside (the other side).

For both White and Black, the names and locations of the files and of Kingside and Queenside happen to be the same and remain so throughout the game. If White chooses to castle (move his King to the) Queenside, that half of the board remains the "Queenside." But reference to the area specifically about the King is made in terms of the King's position, or, technically, "the King field" (the square on which the King stands and those adjacent).

The ranks on the board are numbered from 1 to 8. But, on this point White and Black differ: each side numbers from its own side of the board. Thus, each rank has a dual designation: White's first rank is Black's eighth; White's fourth is Black's fifth. In most chess books when an attack on the opponent's King is brewing, a player's eighth rank is often referred to as "the opponent's back rank," since the opponent generally keeps his King securely back. "The seventh rank" earns frequent mention, too, since the player's action with Rooks, which are particularly effective in sweeping a rank, often takes place there during an attack on the King.

Any square is indicated by reference to its file and rank. Thus, the Queen Rook's square is QR1 for White; but the same square, for Black, is QR8. The fourth square before White's King is K4; for Black, K5, whereas the fourth before *his* King is K4 for him, K5 for White. The context should make clear whether the rank is named from the White or the Black side. But, when such inference cannot readily be made, a good textbook will state explicitly "White's KN6" or "Black's KB4."

Notation of the Chess Moves. Knowing the names of the squares and of the chessmen, the beginner can readily fit them together to indicate, or to describe (in what is aptly known as "Descriptive Notation"), the moves of the men. In the early days of European chess, the notation was lengthy and cumbersome. Moving the King Pawn from its original square one square forward was written out (together with the designation of the number of the move: for instance, first or fifteenth in the game):

1. King Pawn from the second square to the third square before the King.
15. Queen from its first square to the fifth square before the King Rook.

In time, the terms were codified more and more, in effect reduced to a chessic shorthand. The designation of the square whence the man moved was found to be superfluous. The men were represented by symbols (which have been stated previously in this book), and symbols were concocted for the various kinds of moves. The latter symbols are:

- = moves to   0-0 = castles on the Kingside
x = captures   0-0-0 = castles Queenside

Also, "ch" is appended to a move to indicate if a check occurs; "e.p." if a Pawn capture is made "en passant."

Note also that a good move is commonly applauded with a "!"; a bad move with a "?"; a spectacularly good move, as in the initiation of a surprise combination, by a "!!"; a losing move with a "??."

Hence, the first moves of the common opening known as the Ruy Lopez appear as follows:

RUY LOPEZ

WHITE	BLACK
1 P-K4	....

White moves his King Pawn to its fourth rank. (The ellipsis in the second column indicates that Black's move is yet to come.) Then:

1	**P-K4**

Black has made a corresponding move, opposing White head on in the center by moving *his* King Pawn to its fourth rank. (Here the ellipsis, in the first column now, indicates that White's move has already been made.) Other Black moves are possible, of course: 1 ... P-K3 leads generally to the French Defense; 1 ... P-QB4 to the Sicilian Defense; 1 ... P-QB3 to the Caro-Kann, and so on. But to continue:

2 N-KB3	**N-QB3**

Each side has now brought out a Knight: White, his King Knight to the third rank before his King Bishop, or the third square before that Bishop (KB3); Black, his Queen Knight to the third square before his Queen Bishop (QB3). White is attacking and Black defending the Black King Pawn. On the third move we have:

3 B-N5	....

White has advanced his King Bishop. As it is his only movable Bishop, *B* and not *KB* serves notationally here. And, similarly, N5 suffices since KN5 is impossible, and so QN5, the only fifth rank square available, is clearly understood to be meant. (Notation is always expressed in the shortest form possible.)

If the moves we have just covered were to be run

together in a linear style (known as "running notation"), the text would appear as follows: 1 P–K4, P–K4; 2 N–KB3, N–QB3; 3 B–N5 ....

Table of Relative Values

The accent in the study of chess is always on checkmate. This ultimate goal, however, is not generally a matter of dumb luck or an opponent's *fingerfehler* (error). The foundation of a checkmate may be many things. It may be, for example, the tail-end of a combinational foray (series of forcing moves) or of a strategic bind (position which has cramped the opponent's men). And it often is the result of an overwhelming force.

One thing is certain. Material is force, and a preponderance of force brooks little or no interference or resistance. The power of a puny Pawn is generally the primary factor in determining the relative values of the chessmen.

In this connection, the table of relative values of the chessmen is useful. Evaluating a Pawn as a unit of one (and all pieces are valued in relation to the Pawn), the

Illustration 34

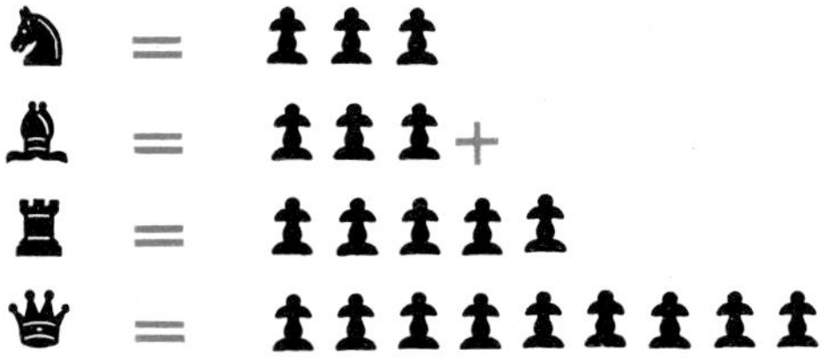

Table of relative values

Knight is the equivalent of three units, the Bishop three and a small fraction, the Rook five, and the Queen nine.

As it is not always possible or even desirable to swap Pawn for Pawn, or Knight for Knight, etc., it is well to calculate in an exchange the value of units given for the value of units received. For example, a player who exchanged two Bishops and a Knight (the unit value of which is 9), or two Knights and a Bishop (unit value also 9), for his opponent's Queen (unit value 9) would be making an even trade, whereas if he traded two Rooks (unit value 10) for that Queen, he would be getting the worst of the deal.

Remember, the gain of material is tantamount to the gain of force, a paramount objective of the game.

Note, however, that these values are both rule-of-thumb and conditional. Thus, at various times in the game, the specific values for the moment vary. In the beginning, on a crowded board, and even later, if the board remains cluttered, the Knight with its power to jump over obstructions may loom as more valuable than the Bishop, while a Rook tucked away in its obscure corner may play no real part at all. And, later in the game, a Pawn advanced almost to queening and, incidentally perhaps, acting like a bone in the opponent's throat, may be almost invaluable. Late in the game, the long range of Bishops, Rooks, and Queen make them powerful in comparison to the Knights, especially on an open board—though even late in the game, a Knight on the scene of a critical action may play a large part (it can hit at squares of both colors, whereas the Bishop cannot). So consider at any time how useful each man may be: generally, Knight, Bishop, and the King (if it can be used safely—as in the endgame with few if any chances of a mate) can "handle" three Pawns, the Rook five, and the Queen nine.

Any man may be, temporarily and for a given action or set of circumstances, nearly indispensable. But, as circumstances can change unforeseeably, the Table of Relative Values is a good standard on which to fall back. And in the opening of the game, any trade of pieces is usually best judged accordingly.

Rules for Conduct

All games and sports have their rules of conduct. What is tolerated, say, in hockey may be penalized in boxing, or vice versa. And, whereas shenanigans and trickery are often applauded in baseball, they are effectively frowned on in tennis. Chess is meant to be the game of the gallant. And whereas "chess swindles" are highly regarded, these, it must be explained, are not overt "swindles" but, rather, within the realm of the player's mental scheming. A chess move may be or may initiate a "swindle," but it does so, for example, by seeming to drive in one direction while really aiming at another. Or a player, in desperate plight, may bluff at an attack— even to the extent of sacrificing a man—knowing that the attack cannot succeed but hoping that, psychologically, his opponent will be stampeded by the display of force. The famous "chess swindles" of Frank J. Marshall, an American chess champion, were essentially just such attacks—attacks which could have been repelled by exact counter moves but which succeeded because the opponent, harried by being put on the defensive, failed to find the correct replies.

Essentially, in chess, a player's conduct must be such as not to harry or distract his opponent. Talking, especially to annoy or distract, is forbidden. Placing a man half on one square, half on another, or other ploys meant to confuse an opponent are likewise tabu. The rules of conduct are set and published by the international world chess federation (*Federation Internationale des Echecs:* FIDE), by national federations, by state and local bodies, and by organizers of specific events (who usually cite the FIDE rules as pertaining, plus perhaps some special rules for the occasion). In all, the volume of such rules is too great to be presented here. One rule, however, must be made clear; it is vital to proper play:

The "Touch-move" Rule. In formal play, the "touch-move" rule must be strictly observed; and, even in the most friendly games, adherence to the rule makes for not only amicable relations, but also rewarding play in the sense that both players justly feel they have "earned" their result and so work harder to improve their game.

The rule runs: a player who touches a man must move it, if he can; a player who sets down and lets go of a man must let that move stand, if it is legal; and a player who touches an opponent's man must capture it, if he can. By extension, if a player, having touched a man, then touches another, the opponent has the right to decide which of the two is to be moved. Also, if a player touches one of his own men and one of the opponent's, he must capture the opponent's with his own touched man, if such a capture is legal. If it is not, then the opponent chooses whether the player is to move his own man or to capture the opponent's if possible (allowing for legality in either instance).

If a player wishes to correct the position of a man, he can avoid the "touch-move" penalty by saying "*J'adoube*" (or "I adjust") before the act of adjusting.

If a player touches a man which cannot legally be moved or thus makes an illegal move, there is no set penalty (the illegal move must be replaced, of course) and he can go on, if it is his turn to move, to make any legal move of his own free choice.

Advice for Effective Play

With 20 possible first moves from which to choose, then 20 for the opponent, and more arising from each move as the position of the chessmen opens up, any one of a billion possible situations may come about within a very few moves. Which are good, which bad? Alas, even the experts are not fully agreed. So how is the beginner to decide?

Actually, he need not, but can enjoy exploring the almost infinite possibilities—at least, at first. Then, lest he become discouraged by constant losses to more knowledgeable opponents, he can resort to some handy maxims. These pithily indicate tried and true methods which aid in conducting chessplay to success. Still, do remember that all maxims have their exceptions. He who perceives that the latter apply in a given situation may score a telling point.

Begin your opening with either 1 P–K4 or 1 P–Q4. You thus prepare more optional moves, several each by your Queen and one Bishop.

Develop (bring out) your men, if possible, with a threat. The onus of defending then restricts your opponent from considering sound plans of his own.

Develop Knights before Bishops. After the first few moves, the short-range Knight has much less of a choice than the long-range Bishop. So it is better to defer the choice for the Bishop till it is clearer just where it will prove most useful. The Knight does well merely in moving toward the center of the board.

Avoid moving the same man twice in the opening, unless of course a profitable gain will accrue. And doubly avoid exchanging a twice-moved man for one just brought out by your opponent: the exchange eliminates your man, wasting the moves expended on it, and brings forward the new man of your opponent's which recaptures.

That process is known as a *tempo* gain for your opponent. A "tempo" is the time expended in moving a man. You have expended at least two *tempi* (plural of "tempo") previously in bringing your man into position to capture and another in capturing; your opponent's recapturing man represents at least one *tempo* on the board; you have wiped out three of your own. So you have made a present to your opponent of four turns to play!

Do not push forward Pawns haphazardly. They cannot retreat and so any such commitment is permanent and sometimes weakening. Deploy Pawns in the opening, primarily to release pieces such as Bishops and Queen, and simultaneously to contest the center.

Bring out the less valuable pieces first—Knights, then Bishops (generally, and, in a sense, fortunately, the

Rooks cannot come out early). And particularly do not bring out your Queen early because, since it is so valuable, it may be harassed and must run before enemy action.

At all times, seek safety for your King. Castling can be and usually is an effective safety measure.

Always have a purpose in mind when making a move and be sure to understand it, even if it is merely to mark time.

Always try to understand the meaning of your opponent's move. If he is planning a bad maneuver, do not make moves which may discourage it. If you see he is planning a good maneuver, make moves to divert or discourage him.

When you are definitely ahead in material, it becomes good strategy to exchange pieces. The absence of enemy reserve force may emphasize the material lead or may enable an extra Pawn to march on down to queen.

When on the attack, however, and especially after sacrificing material to gain that attack, be chary of exchanges. Your reserves may come in to carry the day.

When simply behind in material, hold off from exchanging also. And try, instead, to complicate the game: establish manifold threats and pressures.

Always think ahead and place your men on squares from which they will have future prospects.

Practice makes perfect, and good planning in present games leads to even better plans in future ones. The story is told of a chess buff who inquired of the difference between a master and a grandmaster. "The grandmaster," he was told, "tosses a chessman into the air, and it falls on the right spot."

Control of the Center

There are two disparate types of advantage in chess. One is the material advantage. To be a Pawn ahead, for example, is to have more force to apply. To be a piece ahead is even stronger. The extra material is visible on the board. The other advantage, "positional," is less tangible but none the less real. It is to control or to have greater control of vital squares on the board, in short, to be able to apply your force more effectively.

Because the material is visible, your efforts to win it are necessarily more obvious. But, when foiled in your more obvious efforts, you can resort to the less obvious—or better yet, be striving for both, ready to take whichever plum falls into your hands. But what is this intangible plum you seek? Which are the vital squares?

There are 64 squares on the board. Half are White, half Black. Except for the colors, they are to all intents and purposes very much alike. Or are they? The truth is that the importance of the squares varies during any game. Since mate is all-important, the King's position is a main consideration: safety and defense for your King; attack and mate for the opponent's. So the squares of the King's field are vital. Similarly, when a mating attack is not feasible, attack on some lesser object may be called for, and then the squares relating to that target become extra-important. At the start of a game, however, you cannot know surely where the opponent's King will be—it presumably will castle, either Kingside or Queenside, but it may not. Nor do you yet know where targets will appear.

Even so, however, some squares are more important than others. The squares in the center of the board, for example, are definitely more important. The reason is crystal-clear when one considers the board in terms of a network of interlinked paths. The Knight, for example, strikes at eight squares from the center of the board; only two from a corner. The Bishop may course from one corner to the opposite; but, to do so, it must traverse the center. The center then is the hub of the network. And the player who controls that hub can send his men from one side of the board to the other with ease. The player who does not control the hub must dispatch his men via devious and time-consuming routes. The man which requires three and four moves, back, across, and up again, to reach a critical point of conflict loses *tempi* to the opposing man which gets there in one or two moves. He loses, in effect, two turns or more to play —and almost surely arrives too late.

As a matter of good strategy, therefore, concentrate on controlling the center right from the start. That is

Illustration 35

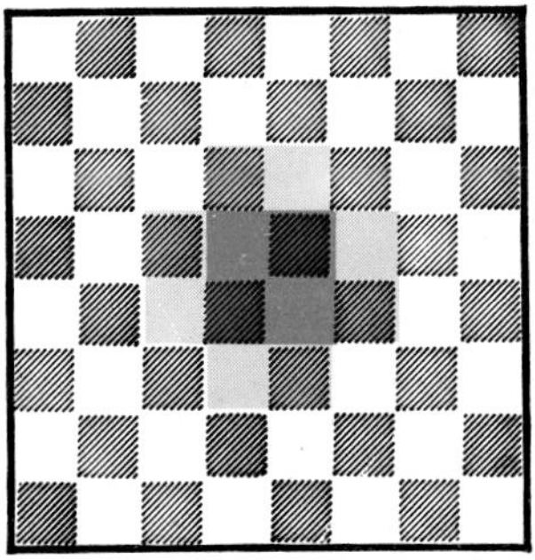

Control the center!

the primary positional advantage to seek in the opening. It enhances your operating space, and hence your mobility, and deters your opponent.

For the opening, the most important squares are the very centermost: K4, Q4, K5, and Q5. You cannot hope, against any reasonably intelligent opponent, to control all. But you fight for your share; and, from that fight, you extend efforts to control your K B4 and/or QB4, and, if possible, your KB5 or QB5, meanwhile guarding zealously your K3 and Q3.

King Safety

To recapitulate for the beginner: the last word, and the first, is to *checkmate the opposing King*. Always, once and for all, the primary object of the game is the opposing King. According to the rules of chess, the King can never be captured: the moment its capture is ensured, it is "checkmated," and the game is over.

It follows, therefore, that a parallel consideration is the safety of your own King. When your King is attacked (checked), it is mandatory to save it.

There are three ways to void a check:

1) capture the attacking man;

2) shield your King by interposing another of your men;

3) move your King "out of check."

Note, moreover, that when the King moves out of check, it must be truly *out*. The King cannot move *into* check; thus, it cannot capture an attacker which is protected by another of the attacking men. Nor can it move to another square which is controlled (attacked) by an enemy man. Generally, however, the King can escape a check if any adjacent square is free from enemy attack (it can even capture the checking man if it is adjacent and unprotected).

When it is possible to interpose one of your other men, that may be the best remedy against a check—especially if the man interposed cannot be captured or is less valuable than the checking man. And the remedy may be particularly fortunate if the man interposed simultaneously gives check (in this case known as "cross-check") to the opponent's King.

The very best remedy is to capture the checking man—when that method serves to ward off the attack permanently and does not concede too valuable a man to the opponent.

In a pinch, however, the check must be voided no matter what the cost!

Consequently, it is best of all to foresee and avoid or prevent all attacks on your King. Such forethought is what is really meant by "King safety."

The chief means to secure King safety is to mobilize (bring out) your men promptly in the opening. They serve to ward off attacks. Next clear the space between your King and a Rook quickly, and then castle, since the center files are usually more subject to attack. Meanwhile, conserve and keep back the Pawns on the wing to which you plan to move your King in castling. For the Pawns serve as a flexible and "inexpensive" barrier against enemy attacks.

Castle, however, if you must or if you will, but not simply because you can. If threatened by attack, you may have to castle as best and as fast as you can. If at a loss for any other constructive move, you may wish to castle and can well do so if the wing to which your King goes seems safe. But, given time or choice, consider carefully. Plan to castle where the opponent does not have forces directed: where he cannot readily bring Rooks to bear on opened files or a Bishop on an open or openable diagonal. And, if you see the possibility of storming the opposing King on one flank, aim to castle your King on the other—especially if your attack entails advancing your own Pawns.

Finally, when castled or planning to castle, have a force of defending men, at least three Pawns and a Knight, stationed as a ready guard.

Sample Checkmates

Illustrations 36 to 40 present more or less common-place checkmates—settings in which the King is so attacked it cannot escape danger by capturing the attacking piece, or by stepping out of all lines of fire, or by interposing a friendly piece.

In illustration 36 the Black King is in the direct line of fire of the White Rook. Black is without resource: he can neither capture the attacker, interpose on the line of fire, or step out of it. Thus, the Black King is checkmated and the game is over. White wins.

In illustration 37 White has a plethora of pieces as a material lead. But they do him no good since he is checkmated. His King is in the line of fire of Black's Bishop on the long diagonal, and no defensive resource is available.

Illustration 36

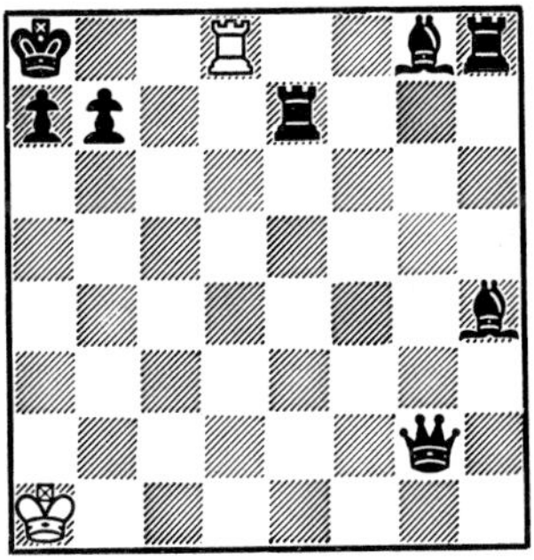

Illustration 37

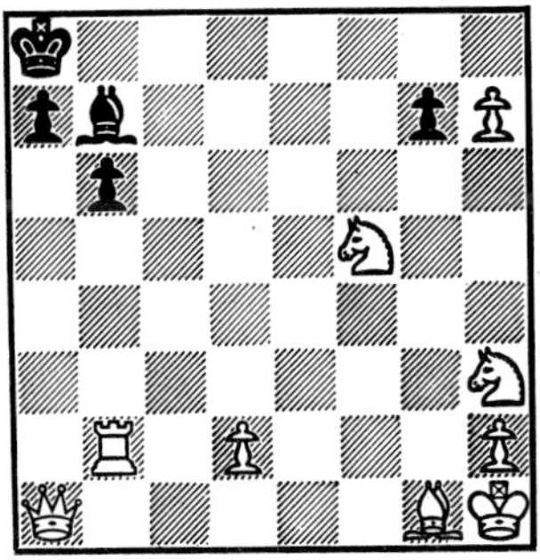

Illustration 38

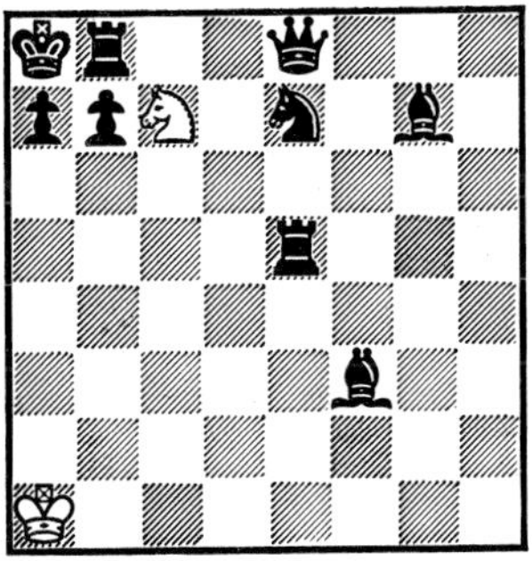

Illustration 39

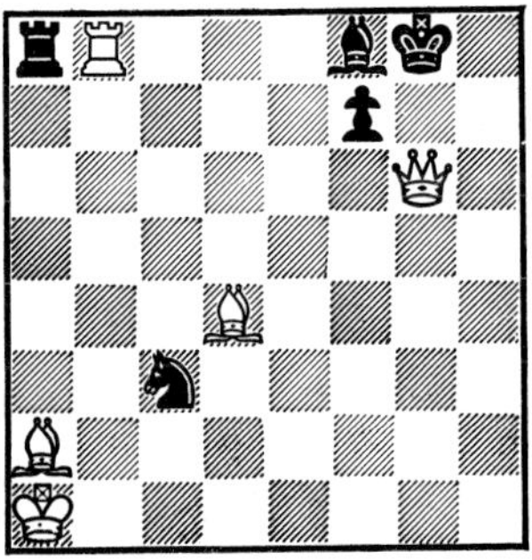

Illustration 38 displays one of the less usual finishes. The Black King, surrounded and blocked by its own two Pawns and a Rook, is attacked by a White Knight. Black is checkmated. This windup is known as a smothered mate.

The situation in illustration 39 has a number of complexities about it. White's Queen is directly attacking the Black King, and Black is without resource. Black cannot capture the Queen with his Pawn for, in doing so, he exposes his King to the fire of one White Bishop. Nor

can Black interpose his Bishop to intercept the check. If
the Bishop moves, Black's King is exposed to the line of
fire of White's Rook, making the play illegal. And there
is no way for Black's King to walk into safety (White's
other Bishop commands the corner square). Thus, Black
is mated.

Illustration 40

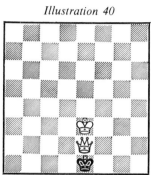

The position in illustration 40 occurs frequently at the
tailend of a beginner's game. Because the Black King
cannot get out of the line of fire of the hostile Queen and
cannot capture the Queen, Black is checkmated.

Drawn Games

In chess, not all games are won. A game may be called
"drawn" under certain circumstances.

Draw by Agreement. Both sides may conclude that a win
is not feasible for any of various reasons such as lack
of time, lack of mating power left on the board, or even
(admitted) lack of ability, if not to mate, then to outplay
the opponent. (Rules at a particular, formal tournament
generally require that both sides exert a minimum

effort—for instance, make 31 moves—before so agreeing. In an informal, sociable game, the players may so agree at any time.)

Draw by the 50-move Rule. When a player whose turn it is to move can prove that at least 50 moves have been made without a man having been captured or a Pawn having been moved, he can claim the game is drawn. (There are some rare positions for which this rule does not hold since mate can occur only after more than 50 such moves.)

Draw by Repetition of Position. When precisely the same position occurs three times in a game with the same player about to move each time, either player can claim that the game is drawn, provided he does so before another move is made. (The right to claim is restored if the same position comes up again.)

Draw by Stalemate. When a player whose turn it is to move and whose King is not then in check cannot make a legal move, the game is drawn. (Usually, such a circumstance comes about by oversight on the part of the superior side. But, occasionally, the losing side can find a move which brings about a Stalemate by force.)

Draw by Perpetual Check. When one player can check literally *ad infinitum* and proves he can do so, the game is drawn. (Usually, of course, it is a player who would otherwise lose the game who wants the "perpetual." On comparatively rare occasions, the "perpetual" works because, if the checking man is captured, then that player's King is stalemated.)

Draw by Exhaustion of Forces. When the men on both sides have been exchanged to the point that neither has force enough left to effect a checkmate (for instance,

King against King; King and Knight against King; King and Bishop against King; King and two Knights against King; or King, Bishop, and a Rook Pawn which cannot be forced through to queen against King), then the outcome must be a draw.

Reasons for Draws. There are any number of reasons why a player may prefer to have to accept a draw. Winning the game is of course his goal, and a drawn game is, as in the French term for it (*nulle partie*), in effect no game. It is, as an amateur once put it: "All that effort for nothing!"

Most of the reasons for draws are implicit in the foregoing definitions of the types of draws. But in any game in which one player has anticipated victory, he is naturally unhappy only to draw, and his opponent is particularly pleased if he manages by a ruse to avert the loss, and sometimes outright gleeful when the player inadvertently or carelessly "blunders" into a drawn position.

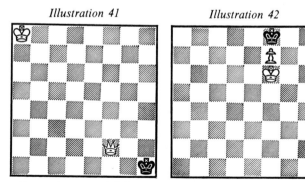

Illustration 41

Illustration 42

**Drawn by an oversight—
with Black to move**

**An inevitable draw—
with Black to move**

When two players have battled to a draw "by exhaustion of forces," there is usually valid reason for mutual congratulations. But many draws come about by careless inadvertence, against which a winning player must guard. And some, still with the element of carelessness, permit the losing player to perpetrate a saving ploy.

In illustration 41, White has, as will be seen (under "Mop-up Campaigns," page 71), ample means for winning the game, but they avail him naught as he has set Black's King without a legal move. Result: stalemate, and a draw.

Illustration 42 shows a position typical of a race to queen a Pawn when the opposing King can reach the square on which the Pawn is to queen. Again, a stalemate draw.

In illustration 43, peculiar circumstances conjoin (with Black to move) to bring about a Stalemate. Black's Knight cannot move without exposing its King to check; his Bishop is in like plight; and his King has no move.

Illustration 43

**An abnormal draw—
with Black to move**

Illustration 44

**White to move
and draw**

In illustration 44, White faces a sure loss on 1 QxR or 1 K-N3 or N2, RxQch, as the Black Pawn on the Queen Knight file then goes on to queen. But White can opportunely play 1 K-R4! and save his game by drawing. For then 1 ... RxQ leaves White without a legal move, a Stalemate.

In illustration 45, White's Queen is checking and can continue to check Black's King *ad infinitum*, by 1 ...

<table>
<tr><td>*Illustration 45*</td><td>*Illustration 46*</td></tr>
</table>

A perpetual check   **Perpetual check or stalemate**

K–B1; 2 Q–B3ch, K–N1; 3 Q–N3ch, K–R1; 4 Q–R6ch, K–N1; 5 Q–N3ch, etc. Black's King cannot escape from the end rank, and no pieces can interpose on checks nor capture the Queen.

In illustration 46, Black is in an apparently hopeless position but, on the move, has a saving clause: 1 . . . R–R7ch! Then 2 KxR leaves Black without a legal move: Stalemate! And 2 K–N1, R–N7ch; 3 K–B1, R–B7ch can run the White King across the board and back for a Perpetual Check, while any KxR sets up Stalemate again.

A Recheck on Checks

Solutions on page 156.

Illustration 47   *Illustration 48*

1. In illustration 47, if it were Black's move, there would be eight different ways for him to check White's King. Do you see them?

2. In illustration 48, White's King is in check. Obviously, then, it is White to move. In how many ways is it possible to get out of check?

3. The position in illustration 49 is deceptive. It is White's turn to move, and he plays his Queen to the last rank, as indicated, thinking he is delivering a checkmate. But is his play legal?

Illustration 49

Point of Summation

At this point, the beginner who has read this book attentively and absorbed the contents in detail has all he needs to know to become a chessplayer. How good a chessplayer he may become depends on how well he applies his knowledge.

On the ensuing pages, he will find some elaboration and extension of the preceding materials, some suggestions and guidance as to how to apply his knowledge, and some practical exercises for developing his chessic abilities.

Also, these following lessons will help to familiarize him with reading chess notation.

For the moment, however, it is important that he be sure he has thoroughly absorbed the preceding lessons. He can test his comprehension by taking the following quiz.

Summary Quiz

1. Name the pieces White may move on his first turn.
2. On his first turn, White has the choice of how many moves?

3. In answer to any first move by White, how many possible replies has Black?

4. What piece combines the powers of the Rook and Bishop?

5. What piece combines the powers of the Rook and Knight?

6. What piece combines the powers of the Bishop and Knight?

7. Name three possible ways to get a King in "check" out of check.

8. What is the result if the King cannot get out of check?

9. A check by two different men does not lend itself to interposition. Which are the men?

10. What happens when a player's King moves into the line of fire of an enemy piece?

11. What happens when the White King moves to the square adjacent to the Black King?

12. If a player illegally moves a piece, what is to be done?

13. If a player touches an enemy piece, what is the rule?

14. When a player advances a Pawn to the eighth rank, what is the status of the Pawn?

15. How many Queens may a player have on the board at the same time?

16. What is meant by "castling"?

17. Which is generally the more powerful, Rook or Bishop?

18. Place a Knight on a central square of an uncluttered board. How many squares does it command?

Solutions on page 157.

Part II
Rebegin at the Beginning

Now the reader knows all the moves and the rules of chess. He stands at the fountainhead of a most fascinating and tantalizing pastime. The 64 squares and their enchanted men are ready.

First, however, he must learn to think for himself. Shall he begin to move aimlessly—hit or miss—employing merely nonsense maxims such as "Always check, it may be mate"? Or shall he embark upon a study of strategy and tactics, grand plans, minor plans, feints, traps, pitfalls, retreats, advances, diversions, blockades, defenses, exchanges, sacrifices, deployments, advanced posts, combined operations, and a host of schemes and procedural forays?

One thing at a time. Logically, strange as it may seem, the learner should begin with the ending! For there he has but a few units to manipulate and obviously can manage them more readily than all 32 men. Psychologically, however, he is not yet attuned to such disciplined pressure. He insists upon commanding all the forces, even while he is not able.

Well, he ought to cater to his intoxication. He *should* command all the forces. And he can do so, marshalling the entire armies, in the following examples, and yet glean lessons which are essential to a further understanding of the game.

The Fool's Mate

The game is about to begin. The players check the setup of the board and the setting of the men. There is a white square at the right-hand corner for each contender, according to the laws of chess. And each man is located exactly where it ought to be. Particular note is made of the placement of the respective Queens. Each is on its color; the White Queen on a white square, and at the opposite end of the same file on a black square, the Black Queen.

Illustration 50

The first player has a choice of 20 different moves. The King, Queen, Bishops, and Rooks cannot move. No paths have been cleared for them. So the choice is limited to one of 16 different Pawn moves (two for each of eight Pawns and one of four different Knight moves (two for each Knight).

White moves first, according to the laws of chess.

And he plays 1 P–KB4.

1   P–KB4   . . . .

The King Bishop Pawn moves from King Bishop 2 to King Bishop 4.

Illustration 51 shows the movement. The White Pawn now is on King Bishop 4. Its original square is marked by a star.

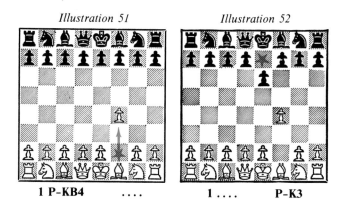

Illustration 51	*Illustration 52*
1 P–KB4	**1** **P–K3**

While a master player may find a reason for making this first move, the learner makes the move for no valid reason. He is playing hit or miss, at random, and is pleased that he is able to make a legal move.

Actually, more will be known about White's first move as White becomes conversant with principles.

1 ....   **P–K3**

For his first move, Black plays 1 ... P–K3.

Black had a choice of 20 different replies—two moves each with eight different Pawns and two moves each with two different Knights. There are a number of reasons, valid and otherwise, why the move in illustration 52 might be selected. But the likelihood here, since the player of the Black forces is an absolute beginner, is that Black's move was a matter of chance. Black may even have touched his King Pawn and, realizing he was playing touch-move, moved the Pawn.

Often, moves made without hesitation, without a moment's thought, turn out to be good and, conversely, sometimes engrossing calculations produce foolish or wasted moves.

    2 P-KN4   ....

For his second move, White plays 2 P-KN4.

Illustration 53   *Illustration 54*

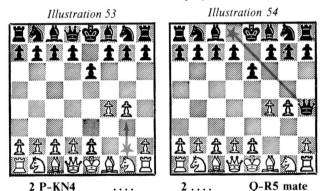

2 P-KN4   ....   **2 ....**   **Q-R5 mate**

The only excuse for White's second move is the law of inertia: "A body in motion tends to remain in motion. . . ." White previously advanced his Bishop Pawn and no harm came of it, so he now advances his King Knight Pawn, feeling quite satisfied with himself.

In fact, White has just invited checkmate!

    2 ....   **Q-R5 mate**

Lulled into a sense of confidence by the apparent simplicity of his first two moves, White now awakens to his sad plight (see illustration 54).

White's King is attacked, and is in check. It cannot move out of check, largely because its own men hem it in. No White man can be interposed between Black's Queen and the King. And no White man is in position to capture the checking Queen.

Though Black is a beginner, too, the opportunity is too clear to miss. The game ends swiftly as Black declares checkmate.

The Scholar's Mate

As is customary, White makes the first move.

1   P-K4   ....

Illustration 55

1 P-K4   ....

The King Pawn moves from King 2 to King 4.

The players, White and Black, are conversant by now with a few principles. White advances his King Pawn two squares to free his King Bishop and his Queen for future action. At the same time, the move commands

Illustration 56   *Illustration 57*

1 ....   P-K4   2 B-B4   ....

the central square Q5 and the near-central square KB5.
Academically, all is well and good.

1 ....   P-K4

Black's King Pawn moves from his K2 to his K4.

Black evidently reasons that what is good enough for
White is good enough for Black. (Though this line of
reasoning may serve well here, it is not always reliable.)
The advance of Black's King Pawn two squares also frees
his King Bishop and Queen for future action. And his
move, 1 ... P-K4, also commands the central square,
Black's Q5 and the near-central square, Black's KB5.
Here, too, all is well.

2 B-B4   ....

White moves his King Bishop to Queen Bishop 4.

Note that in expressing this move it is not necessary
to say KB-QB4, or King Bishop to Queen Bishop 4.
Since the only Bishop that can move at the moment is
the King Bishop, the reference to the Bishop move must
necessarily pertain to the King Bishop. And since the

only Bishop square to which the Bishop can go is Queen Bishop 4, it is not necessary to define the exact movement. B–B4 is quite exact under the circumstances.

At this point, White has a wide choice of moves and patterns. There is no telling why he selects this move. He may be following general principles. One principle, for example, is to put your men to work or, in other words, develop your men so that they will be in position to work. Another principle is to place your men so that they will control the center. Here White's Bishop controls the important central square Q5. Also, incidentally, its line of fire includes Black's square KB2, a critical square as it is within the "King's field."

2 ....   **B–B4**

Illustration 58

2 ....   **B–B4**

Black moves his King Bishop to Queen Bishop 4.

The same points made for White in expressing his move also hold good for Black.

Black selects this move for any number of reasons. He may know the anticipated pattern, for example,

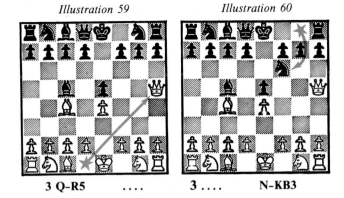

Illustration 59 *Illustration 60*

3 Q-R5 .... 3 .... N-KB3

better than he knows other patterns. Or he may use the earlier line of reasoning: "If it's good enough for White, it is good enough for Black." Or he may rely on its theoretical background: The illustrated move develops a piece and it controls the central square, Black's Q5. Incidentally, mirroring White's move, it too is directed toward a critical square, White's KB2.

3   Q-R5   ....

White moves his Queen to Rook 5.

White's move, strictly on academic grounds, can'be found wanting. For one thing, it can be shown that White's Queen is exposing itself to attack and, in the process of repelling the Queen, Black will gain time.

But White's move must not be discounted entirely. It evokes the germ of an idea. White is putting a diabolical scheme to work. He is threatening checkmate and hoping his opponent will not see the threat.

3   ....   N-KB3

Black replies by developing his King Knight.

It is often the case that a player whose mind is stuffed with general principles overlooks the simplest. Here Black brings out his King Knight; for in doing so, he attacks his adversary's Queen. By rights, the attack on the Queen should gain him time. And, if there were any justice in chess, this counter-attack, instead of a passive defense, should earn a reward.

4   QxBP mate

Illustration 61

4 QxBP mate

White plays 4 QxBP and delivers checkmate.

Yes, there is justice in chess. Often, a player makes 39 good moves and one bad one and loses. Here, though Black vaguely knew principles, he overlooked the primary point of the game, a checkmate. And checkmate is the end.

Black's King is attacked by the enemy Queen and cannot get out of attack by capture, interposition, or escape. The game is over.

This is the Scholar's Mate. It is the scholar who, crammed with one hundred and one principles, would overlook or forget the first: checkmate.

Mop-up Campaigns

There are many simple endings common to chess which every beginner ought to understand. One of these is King and Queen vs. King—a powerfully unbalanced force where the dynamic difference between both sides is so great that the question of winning or checkmating is hardly relevant. The superior side will always succeed if he knows the simple technique.

But first the learner must know that, according to the rules of the game, checkmate must be administered in 50 moves or less. Else the game will be declared a draw.

Illustration 62

**An example of King and Queen
vs. King**

King and Queen vs. King. In the application of the winning technique, moreover, the superior side, curiously, must exercise caution. An excess of force spells danger—here, the danger of stalemate.

White's general plan is to confine the enemy King to an edge or corner of the board. For checkmate cannot be effected on open terrain.

1 Q-Q1   ....

This move is not the only way for White to achieve his goal. An alternate way would be to drive Black's King to a corner or edge with the assistance of the White King. But the move is eminently sufficient. The main point is that it restricts the movement of the Black King.

The Black King is confined now within the limits of the four kingside files. And Black must move. He tries to put up as much resistance as he can—though knowing it is in vain.

1 ....   **K-K3**

Here, too, White has a wide choice. But he brings his King toward the center of the board.

2 K-N7   ....

White does so because he needs the cooperation of his King and Queen in checkmating. And Black, stubbornly fighting, tries to hold in the center.

2 ....   **K-K4**

Even though eventually Black will have moved in vain, he resists in hope of an error by his opponent.

3 K-B6   ....

And Black gives ground.

3 ....   **K-K3**

The Kings are now squarely opposed with but one square between them, a situation in which they are said to be in "opposition." White is thus in position to restrict the mobility of the Black King still further.

4 Q-K2ch   ....

Black must skirt the edge.

4 ....   **K-B4**

White now usurps the more important central terrain.

5 K-Q6   ....

And Black is driven closer to the Queen.

| 5 .... | K-B5 |

The alternatives, 5 ... K-N3 or 5 ... K-N4 fail against, say, 6 Q-B3. After 5 ... K-B3, the Kings would again be in "opposition," and then 6 Q-B3ch would force Black's King to the King Knight file. Now White closes in.

| 6 K-Q5 | .... |

There follows:

6	K-B4
7 Q-B3ch	K-N4
8 K-K6	K-N3
9 Q-N3ch	K-R4
10 K-B6	K-R3

Now White has a choice of four checkmates: They are 11 Q-N6 mate, 11 Q-R2 mate, 11 Q-R3 mate, and 11 Q-R4 mate.

In the foregoing play, after White played 8 K-K6, Black might have set a trap with 8 ... K-R5, instead of 8 ... K-N3. See illustration 63.

Illustration 63

Black has set a trap

Now, on 9 K̇–B6 (or 9 K–B5), which has the earmarks of the correct move since it closes in on Black's King, White is the victim. He has carelessly stalemated his opponent. (See illustration 64).

Black's King is not attacked. But he has no legal move. The game is a draw.

Illustration 64   *Illustration 65*

Stalemate!   **An example of King and Rook vs. King**

King and Rook vs. King. Here, too, the learner must remember that checkmate must be administered in 50 moves or less, according to the rules of the game. Else the game will be declared a draw.

Here, in the application of the winning technique, it is still necessary to exercise caution. For the danger of stalemate is less, but not negligible. Accuracy and precision, moreover, are necessary to expedite the mating process. (See illustration 65.)

Time may be saved if the learner is conversant with the method and some details. To begin with, he ought to know that a King and Rook cannot mate the enemy King in the center of the board. The target King must be on the edge or corner. Then he can be tracked down and checkmated. Observe illustrations 66 and 67.

Illustration 66

Illustration 67

The target Black King is trapped on the edge of the board. With White to move, checkmate ensues "by force." See how?

The target Black King is trapped in the corner. Here, with either side to move, checkmate ensues "by force"

The illustrative examples show the only mating "nets" (positions in which a King is ensnared for mating) in King and Rook vs. King. In illustration 66, the Black King is trapped on the edge, with White to move.

Hence, White can immediately close the net on Black. He simply plays 1 R–K1, applying the method of forcing the opposition, Black's only reply is then 1 . . . K–B1; entering into a position where the King's are juxtaposed to each other, known as opposition.

White then plays 2 R–K8 checkmate.

In illustration 67, Black is trapped no matter who is to move. On the move, White can play at once 1 R–R8 checkmate. With Black to move, Black must play 1 . . . K–N1; whereupon White replies 2 R–R8 checkmate.

Now return to illustration 65 (page 74).

There are usually many alternative ways of limiting the enemy moves. Here White can play, for example, 1 R–Q1. Then on the one side, Black cannot cross beyond the Queen Bishop file. But even more limiting is 1 R–B7. And Black is restrained: he is on the first rank and cannot encroach upon the second rank.

1 R–B7	K–Q1

Black's move is as good as any. No matter, he will eventually be mated.

2 K–N5	K–K1

The Rook is attacked and must move.

3	R–QR7	K–B1
4	K–B6	K–N1
5	K–Q6	K–B1
6	K–K6	K–N1
7	K–B6	K–R1
8	K–N6	K–N1

With the King's in opposition, White administers mate.

9 R–R8 mate.

Forced into the mating net on the corner of the board, Black had no "save."

From these few examples, the chess beginner can and should evolve one main principle for mating endings: when the forces on the board are reduced enough, his own King becomes a vital fighting piece. With King and Queen against a lone King, for example, it is only by the conjoined efforts of his Queen *and* King that he can effect mate.

Occasionally, as in some of the "Sample Checkmates" (page 52), a lone piece can effect a mate; or a Knight or a Pawn may effect a "smothered mate"—but these are all to some extent smothered mates: that is, the opponent's own men so hem in his King, without truly sheltering it, that the King is deprived of "flight" squares and so falls.

In such situations, with pieces and Pawns cluttering the board, the player does best to keep his own King well sheltered lest some surprise check aid his opponent.

When the opponent's pieces are gone, however, or his pieces and Pawns reduced to comparative futility, then the player marches forth his King to join in the battle. For, on a wide-open board, no adverse piece can effect mate by itself, and the King renders essential support, as has just been shown in the endings of King and Queen vs. King, and King and Rook vs. King (pages 71–76).

Thus, too, the King can cooperate with two Bishops or with Knight and Bishop to bring about a mate and may, in many instances, aid in and shorten the mating process with such greater force as Queen and Bishop, Queen and Knight, or Rook with either Bishop or Knight. The process—in the absence of enemy pieces on the board—is always the same: the player's King marches to oppose the opponent's King; the King and pieces conjoin to drive the opponent's King to the edge or corner of the board; and then the pieces close in to effect the mate.

Some typical end (mating) positions are the following: **King and Two Bishops vs. King.** Illustrations 68 and 69 show the end result and a possible beginning of the mating process with King and two Bishops. In illustration 69, the Bishops confine the Black King to the left

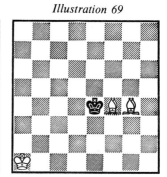

Illustration 68

Illustration 69

Mate by King and Bishops. Note that if White's King were not where it is or on QR6, Black's King would escape via Black's QR2

A prior position. Black's King attacks a Bishop; but, by 1 B-KN3, White saves the Bishop, yet holds his barrier intact

side of the board. After White's 1 B-N3, Black may move his King toward the center, his safest refuge, by 1 ... K-Q4. But, by advancing his King, White soon corners the opposing King, not easily but inevitably. The sequels may vary according to where Black tries to direct his King. But, supposing the Black King runs or is driven to Black's QR1, White mates, as in illustration 68 above, by the simple B-B3.

Ha! But does he, though? The great danger for White in this type of mate is to stumble into Stalemate. Put White's Bishop on B3 in that left-hand illustration back on KN4 and then say what Black's last move could have been! Black had no legal move and was Stalemated! White's mating plan was defective.

His first moves, however, were not necessarily faulty.

One possible sequence to a mate, in illustration 69 (each Black move may lead, of course, to a different one), is 1 B-N3, K-Q4; 2 K-N2, K-K5; 3 K-B3, K-Q4; 4 K-Q3, K-B3; 5 K-B4, K-N2; 6 K-N5, K-R1 and now, not 7 K-N6 Stalemate, but 7 B-B8, K-R2; 8 K-B6, K-R1.

Note how the King and one Bishop serve to box Black's King in the corner, yet leave it two unattacked squares so there is no Stalemate, while the final mate is set up. Now that mate is easy: 9 K-B7, K-R2; 10 B-B2ch, K-R1; 11 B-N7 mate.

Illustration 70   *Illustration 71*

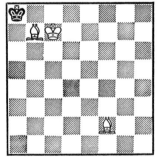   

A true mate
with King and Bishops

No mate is possible.
White cannot mate with
Bishops on the same colored
squares—which he might
have via Pawn promotion.
Here he has no checks
on the white squares!

King, Bishop, and Knight vs. King. With Bishop and Knight, a player can also effect mate with the aid of his King. In illustration 72, 1 N–N6ch, K–R2; 2 N–B8ch, K–R1; 3 B–B6 achieves a typical mating position. Note that the King to be mated must be in, or be driven into, a corner, and it must be a corner assailable by the Bishop.

Illustration 72

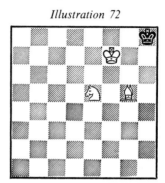

Here, with King, Bishop, and Knight, a forced mate may follow

The mate can be effected from any setup on the board in a maximum of 37 moves. But it is highly technical and an arduous process beyond the proper range of a beginner at chess. Briefly described, the process is to harry the opposing King to the edge of the board and thence to one corner. But a shrewd opponent heads his King for a corner which the player's Bishop cannot assail. The King can be forced thence to a corner of the other color, but only by one of a few methods, each of which is technically very precise and difficult. A single misstep may let the opposing King escape from the edge of the board; and then, unfortunately, it may be impossible to herd the King into a proper corner for mate within the 50 moves permitted.

King and Two Knights vs. King. With no other men on the board, a player cannot normally mate with King and two Knights. True, in illustration 73, White, on the move, does mate, by 1 N–N6. But (as in illustration 68) what was Black's previous move? His King cannot be confined in a corner pending the arrival of the check-mating Knight without first being Stalemated.

A player must be alert, however, and remember that all chess axioms contain an implicit "normally." He should not concede a draw just because his forces have been reduced to King and two Knights. For, when the opponent has another man besides his King, and so is not necessarily subject to or capable of forcing a Stale-mate, the player may yet mate.

In illustration 74, White mates while letting his opponent apparently gain a superiority by queening: 1 N–B3! P–R7; 2 N–R4, P–R8(Q); 3 N–N6 mate.

In illustration 75, White likewise mates even though Black has a Bishop and a Pawn. On 1 N–B3! Black can

Illustration 73 *Illustration 74*

Here the apparent mate   White can mate
is illusory

Illustration 75

White can mate

try 1 ... P–K5; 2 N–R4, B–K4, meaning to swap off White's confining Knight by 3 ... BxN. But White's other Knight arrives in time with 3 N–N6 mate. Or Black can try for 1 ... B–B2; 2 ... B–Q1 and 3 ... BxN; but, again, 3 N–N6 is just in time for mate.

Some mating positions with King and two Knights come about in many more than the 50 moves normally permitted before an opponent can claim a draw. Under the laws of chess, the player with the two Knights can have the extra moves, provided that he is able to prove that he can mate. (This provision is interpreted differently—for instance, with various degrees of latitude by some tournament directors). Again, however, the processes are highly technical and beyond the proper range of a beginner at chess.

Lessons from the Endings

Despite a beginner's natural reluctance to delve into the comparatively humdrum details of endgame play, such practice is vital for him. With all 32 men on the board, complexities obscure the lessons and even the comparative values of the men. True, in a particular opening or middle-game position, it may even be essential to exchange a Bishop for a Knight (even as it is sometimes expedient to sacrifice a Queen). But, other considerations being equal, it is wise to trade the other way and retain one's Bishops, rather than Knights. As the preceding lessons have shown, the Bishops have more "mating power" than Knights. So, if the plots and stratagems of the opening and mid-game fail to achieve a winning advantage, the player who has kept his Bishops has the better chances of winning in the ending.

Pawn Endings

"Pawn play," said an early chess author, Philidor, "is the soul of chess." And a Pawn, largely because it can be promoted, certainly becomes a vital factor in the endgame. The chess beginner must therefore learn some elementary principles of Pawn endings; otherwise, he will fail, in opening play and middle games, to set up winning chances or to avert losing ones.

The Passed Pawn. Any Pawn which can trudge down its file unrestrained by an enemy Pawn on that file or an adjacent one is termed a "passed Pawn." In the early stages of the game, when enemy pieces abound, it may not safely march, but remains even so a latent advantage. Late in the game, it may be the winning factor; for, when it is promoted to a Queen, it brings an overwhelming force onto the board.

In illustration 76, White on the move wins; Black on the move draws. The process of determining if a Pawn can queen is one of simple counting, and the beginner must practice counting till it becomes second nature to him. Try it here. If Black is to move, he marches his King directly to his QN2 and arrives just in time: he captures the Queen on the move after White's P–R8(Q) ch. If White is to move, he pushes his Pawn and it becomes a Queen before the Black King can reach it. Thereafter, he wins much as detailed under "Mop-up Campaigns" (page 71).

Illustration 76

The magic square

As an aid to counting, however, the beginner can avail himself of the principle of the "Magic Square" (pictured in red, above). It is particularly useful in evaluating how dangerous an enemy "passed Pawn" may be (or how advantageous one's own) in the middle game when the actual Pawn race may not yet be practicable—but may become so when, as is almost inevitable, the pieces on the board are traded off.

The "Magic Square" is one with sides equal to the distance of the passed Pawn from its queening square (here QR8). If the opposing King is inside that square, the Pawn cannot, by itself, march on to queen. If the adverse King is well outside the square, the Pawn can, all on its own, win by becoming a Queen. If, as here, the King is one move outside the Magic Square, then the Pawn can queen if White is to move, but it cannot if it is Black's turn to move.

Illustration 77

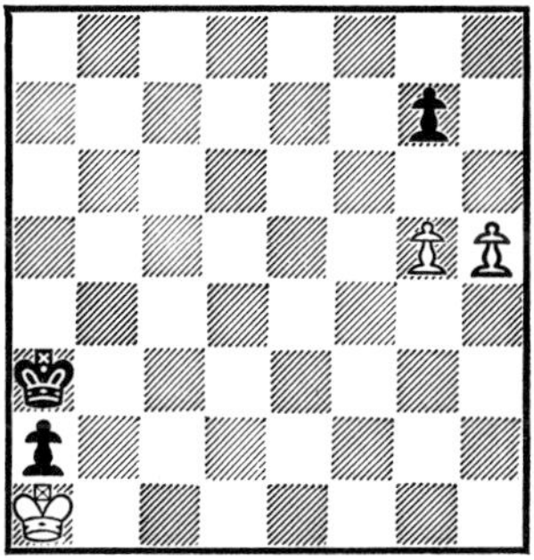

A latent passed Pawn

The Passed Pawn Candidate. The term "Passed Pawn Candidate" applies to a Pawn which can, from a given position, become a passed Pawn. Usually (as in illustration 77), the candidate exists in a position in which a player has more Pawns in a local section than the opponent. Here White has a very perceptible candidate, by 1 P-R6 he immediately has an outright passed Pawn, either by 1 ... PxP; 2 PxP (or even 2 P-N6) or by 1 ... K-N6; 2 PxP (or 2 P-R7), and queens next move. Even if White's Pawns were, however, way back on his

KN2 and KR2, his King Knight Pawn would be a "candidate." Note, however, that then its "candidacy" would be nominal; for Black's King could intervene in time to save a draw—if Black were on the move: 1 ... K–N6; 2 P–R4, K–B5; 3 P–N4, K–Q4; 4 P–R5, K–K4; 5 P–N5, K–B4; 6 P–R6; K–N3; etc. With White on the move, White wins: count out the moves and see.

In illustration 78, White is actually a Pawn behind and his King is confined helplessly—but he can win! The process is a memorable one: 1 P–N6! Now 1 ... P–B3 (or 1 ... P–R3) is futile, as White queens easily after 2 PxRP (or 2 PxBP). But so is 1 ... RPxP (or 1 ... BPxP), as White has the surprising 2 P–B6 (or 2 P–R6) after which a White Pawn becomes passed, no matter how Black replies, and queens in a move or two. And the Queen of course mops up the board and conjoins with its King to mate Black's King.

Of passed Pawns, there are a variety, some stronger than others. From the example just discussed, White emerges with one passed Pawn in some variations,

Illustration 78

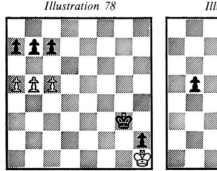

Can White "pass" a Pawn?

Illustration 79

The outside passed Pawn

whereas Black has more. But, except for the blockaded Black Pawn on its KR7, the White one is the *most advanced passed Pawn.* Obviously, a Pawn about to queen is very strong.

In illustration 79, White has what is called the *outside passed Pawn,* sometimes termed the "most outside passed Pawn." Here the Pawns match in number those passed Pawns equally advanced, and Black's King is within the magic square of White's passed Pawn (see page 84). But White wins by 1 P-R5. Now Black can play 1 ... K-K3 to keep within the magic square or 1 ... P-N5 to race for a Queen. But, on 1 ... P-N5; 2 P-R6, P-N6; 3 K-B3, White wins Black's passed Pawn while his "most outside passed Pawn" goes on safely. And, on 1 ... K-K3, White cashes in at once on the latent power of his outside Pawn by 2 K-B5, whereby White's King wins the Black outside passed Pawn, then the other Black Pawn, and escorts his King Pawn on to queen—or the outside Rook Pawn queens.

In illustration 80, White has what is often the strongest

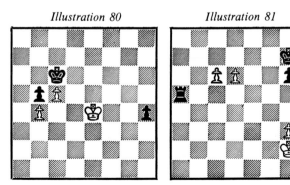

Illustration 80

Illustration 81

The protected passed Pawn

Connected passed Pawns

of all passed Pawns, the *protected passed Pawn*. This example clearly shows why. Despite Black's most outside passed Pawn, White wins, since his King can freely go after that critter, take it, and return: 1 K–B3, P–R6; 2 K–N3, P–R7; 3 KxP, K–Q4; 4 K–N3, K–B3; 5 K–B4, K–Q4; 6 K–B5, K–B3; 7 K–K6, whereupon Black's King must give way as by 7 ... K–B2; 8 K–Q5, K–Q2; 9 P–B6ch, K–B2; 10 K–B5, after which White can take the remaining Black Pawn and then maneuver his King and two Pawns so as to queen and win. All this is possible because if Black deserts White's protected passed Pawn, as by 2 ... K–Q4; 3 K–N4, K–B5, that Pawn placidly moves on to queen: 4 P–B6, etc.

Connected passed Pawns rival the protected passed Pawn in potency. Since one of the passed Pawns can protect the other, at need, the two together can be a winning factor in a game in which all other considerations balance off. And, in illustration 81, for example, they overpower a Rook in the sense that White cannot be stopped from queening.

King and Pawn vs. King. There are many variations even in the ultra simple ending of King and Pawn vs. King. There are two main principles to observe: for the side with the Pawn, the King must normally (that is, unless the Pawn can outrace the opposing King) hasten to support the Pawn; for the defending side, the King must (unless it can capture the Pawn outright) race to guard the square on which the Pawn may queen. Illustration 82 displays the critical position in a close race. The Kings are in "opposition"—that is, directly opposed with but one square between them—so that whichever side has to move, has to give way. If Black has to move, he loses:

e.g. 1 ... K–Q1; 2 K–N7, and the White King protects the Pawn right down to queening. If White has to move, it is a drawn game, provided Black defends correctly: 1 K–Q6, K–Q1; 2 K–B6, K–B1; etc. Or 2 P–B6, K–B1; 3 K–B5, K–B2 (the Black King stays "opposed" to White's whenever possible); 4 K–Q5, K–B1! (4 ... K–Q2 is impossible; and, on 4 ... K–Q1; 5 K–Q6, Black's King has to move out of the "opposition" and loses with 5 ... K–B1; 6 P–B7, K–B2; 7 K–Q7, etc.) and now Black retains the opposition and draws: 5 K–Q6, K–Q1 or 5 K–B5, K–B2.

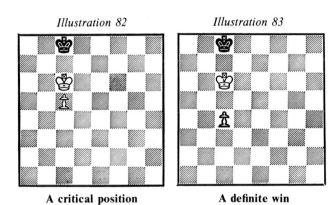

Illustration 82	*Illustration 83*
A critical position	**A definite win**

In illustration 83, White has a win in any event. If it is Black's turn to move, he must yield ground by 1 ... K–Q1 and, after 2 K–N7! K–Q2; 3 P–B5, the Pawn goes through protected. If it is White's turn to move, he has 1 P–B5, whereupon again Black's King must give way, and the Pawn can be protected all the way after either 1 ... K–N1; 2 K–Q7 or 1 ... K–Q1; 2 K–N7.

Part III
Mid-game Tactical Motifs

The game of chess, according to some theorists, is divided into three parts: the opening, the middle game, and the end game. According to others, it is divisible into strategy and tactics or long-range planning and the concrete execution of the goals, the latter usually by means of combinations.

It might seem that strategy is the better part of the whole. For what, pray tell, can override a sound plan? Yet, actually, the result of most games is ascribed to tactics. Myriads of themes govern the tactical format; and these, in combination with each other, deploy an unlimited potential. Even among grandmasters, the outcome of games is attributed 90 percent to tactics.

What is being said here is, in effect, that many a sound plan goes awry by blunders. Nor is this statement simply skeptical. The interstitial, puzzling, and surprising stratagem all too often defeats even the rock-ribbed grand strategy. For it is obvious that, while the deep planner patiently plods through his 49 or 87 would-be perfect moves which will culminate in the strategic victory, he may well, and too often does, overlook the one sly move which can overturn his plan—and the game.

So it is all-important that the student of chess familiarize himself with the following tactical motifs, and extend his knowledge of their intermixtures—which run into the hundreds, if not thousands. Practice on many leads to a sharpening of the eye for many more. And they will give him an unyielding initiative which will win games and, to boot, be fun.

The Elements:
Strong Moves and Double Attacks

Essential to the spirit of tactical play is a knowledge of the strong moves in chess. For some moves are stronger than others.

When one gets down to particular cases, of course, any one move may be the winning move in that particular position. So it is, for that position, the strong move, of whatever kind it may be. It may even be a quiet, "positional" move which, without any overt threat, simply consolidates the position for an ultimate win—in short, just the next step in a long-range plan. Speaking generally, however, there are moves which exert special force in a tactical or near-tactical sense. And it is these which are meant here under the term, "Strong Moves." **Developing Moves.** First to arise in any game are the developing moves, those which deploy the forces for action. In the opening, any first move develops to some extent. But, in considering strong moves, we may discard some and focus on others. Neither tactical nor positional considerations as yet exist as White considers his first move. They arise only after development has begun to shape up. But both players must be looking forward to them.

Illustration 84   *Illustration 85*

Choosing a first move   **Seeking a dual objective**

In illustration 84, White can choose from any of 20 first moves. We discard 1 P-QR3: it promotes no development, and the Rook is not likely to be more useful at QR2; indeed, it may prove an obstruction since the Queen Knight and (later) the Queen Bishop are denied access to QR3. Contrariwise, 1 P-K4 opens four possible moves for the Queen and five for the King Bishop. Also it contests the center; and, while the center is largely a positional consideration, it does bear on tactics. For, in a well conducted game, the first clashes will occur there, and the men in the center will have the first tactical opportunities.

In the right-hand diagram above, White has played 2 N-KB3, a strong developing move since it serves a three-fold purpose. It develops the short-stepping Knight to a square from which it can do most: it contests the center and simultaneously attacks Black's King Pawn, and it executes a step in another project (to be explained).

Black's most logical reply is 2 N-QB3, which serves

an at least dual purpose: developing a short-stepping Knight and protecting the King Pawn, while contesting the center. Then, however, White has 3 B–N5, again with a three-fold purpose: it renews the attack on the Black King Pawn by the threat to eliminate the defending Knight; it develops a piece; and, as is now apparent, it clears the way for White to castle, a convenience which Black cannot yet enjoy.

Note the emphasis on dual and multiple purposes. Any move which actually (not illusorily) accomplishes more than one function is stronger than one which achieves only a single objective. Note, too, that White's N–B3 and B–N5, by attacking and threatening Black's King Pawn, restrict Black to a somewhat limited choice of moves.

In all of this, there is, to be sure, a commingling of tactical and positional considerations. That must be until the deployment of the men, White's and Black's, takes on more definite characteristics. Later, perhaps, the players may both be restricted to purely positional moves—or one or the other may find an opportunity for a tactical surprise move.

Note, too, that attention has been paid to the options permitted by some of these developing moves. The developing move is stronger if it clears the way for other moves by the same side. It is stronger still if it restricts the opponent's choice of moves, as by attacking a man, or the center. It may also be stronger if it induces a move which cuts the options for the opponent. Thus, if Black replies to White's 2 N–KB3 by 2 ... P–Q3 to protect his King Pawn, he has reduced the possible moves for his King Bishop.

Then, too, a developing move is stronger if it augments the player's game positionally. That White can castle after 3 B–N5 is, strictly speaking, a positional advantage—in that it is long-range planning rather than an immediate threat to gain material. But it may also be thought of as "defensive tactics," for, with the King safely removed from the immediate action (remember the chapter on "King Safety," page 50), White enjoys further freedom for conducting tactical operations.

Moves Which Smite. Certain moves exert what is almost a purely tactical force. Such moves so "smite" the opponent that he must consider them and react. First of these, perhaps, is the capture. Next is the check. And third is the threat: threat to mate, threat to capture, and, sometimes, even threat to check. The value of these moves is the compulsion which they exert on the opponent. In a tactical sense, any and all such moves are good when and if they compel the opponent to one restricted, foreseeable, and comparatively innocuous reply. And they may still be good if they limit him to a small number of replies.

One general objective of tactics is to restrict the opponent, to throw a monkey wrench into whatever plans he may have been brewing. Another objective is so to restrict his replies that, in the outcome, he will have lost something—and a chess master may often initiate a whole series of tactical moves, technically known as a "combination," merely to emerge with a better position. Finally, of course, and whenever possible, such a combination is launched to win material or, the ultimate goal, to effect checkmate.

When the latter possibilities are clearly obtainable, no

more need be said: the player launches into tactics. But, as acquaintance with the mysteries and fascinations of chess improves, the beginner will find that chess is a game of exceptions. And the whole range of tactical motifs which, after all, comprise "surprise" moves, also opens a sometimes bewildering possibility of counter surprises.

Hence the beginner must study his every move, and the possible replies to it by his opponent. There is no outright magic even in the moves which smite. They are tools to be used judiciously. A capture which restricts the opponent to a poor recapture is good; one which merely brings forward the opponent's recapturing piece may be downright bad. A check is obviously an error when the checking piece can be captured, or, less obviously, if it is easily parried or evaded. And an ill-considered threat, whether to capture or even to mate, may be futile or worse if it can easily be parried or, as it may sometimes be, simply ignored.

The Double Attack. The best assurance a player can have that his strong move is truly strong is to see that it achieves or at least threatens to achieve more than one objective. A developing move can seldom actually attack two targets at once—but then, as we have said, development is only partially tactical. In the realm of the purely tactical, however, it is the double (or multiple) attack which is most likely to prevail. The "move which smites" attacks but may be countered. The move which smites *doubly* is apt to win something. (We use the word "apt," here, because there is always the possibility of "counter attack" to be considered before making even what appears to be the strongest of attacks.)

Illustration 86

A winning double attack

Here in elementary form is a winning double attack. The White Queen smites (checks) the King and smites (attacks) the Rook. The King must move, the Rook falls.

Illustration 87

A double attack refuted

Here, with a Pawn less, Black has a surprise defense: a winning crosscheck, 1 ... Q–N2ch. After White's forced trade of Queens, Black wins easily.

There remains one word more to say of "strong moves." The ultimate essence is attack. But the quality of the attack must be considered. Of two moves which smite, that which attacks the opponent's more valuable man is qualitatively stronger; strongest is that which threatens to give up the least valuable of the player's men for the most valuable of the opponent's. Hence, a check (attack on the King) or a threat to mate is the most compelling attack; an attack on a Queen, the next. But an attack by a Rook on a protected Queen is not so forcible as an attack on an unprotected Rook. (Consult "The Table of Relative Values," page 41). And, as always, beware of illusions. First, be sure the attack has teeth!

Illustration 88

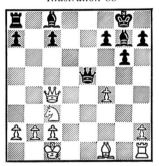

An illusory attack

In illustration 88, White's Pawn attack on the Queen assails the most powerful target piece, but is quite illusory. Black replies with 1 ... B-KR3; the Pawn cannot now leave its position between Black's Bishop and its own King to capture the Queen; and Black ultimately wins the would-be attacker: 2 N-K2, B-N5 and so forth.

Illustration 89

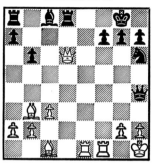

A plethora of illusions

In illustration 89, Black's attack on the Queen is illusory as . . . RxQ would be followed by R–K8 mate. The way in which White wins, however, is subject to further illusions. 1 P–N3 seems to drive Black's Queen from the protection of the Rook on Q1 (as by 1 . . . Q–R6 or N5; 2 QxR mate); but, after 1 . . . B–N2ch! Black validates his attack on the White Queen and, after 2 K–N1, QxPch; 3 KxQ, RxQ has even won a Pawn. Also, the seemingly powerful double attack by 1 Q–QB6, threatening mate after 2 R–K8ch, and also 2 QxR, is negated by the simple 2 . . . B–Q2, whereupon Black may even take over the attack. And 1 R–K4 looks very powerful (1 . . . QxR; 2 QxRch, etc.), but it is countered by the developing move, 1 . . . B–N5, with validation of the attack on White's Queen.

Note, however, that a piece still undeveloped in the middle game is anathema. Black's last counter was to bring out an undeveloped piece. So try the same for White. 1 BxN trades off an undeveloped piece for a developed one with great effect here: on either 1 . . .

PxB or 1 ... B–N2; BxPch, White soon mates (1 ...
B–N2; 2 BxPch, K–R1; 3 BxPch, KxB; 4 Q–K5ch,
etc.). And, on 1 ... B–K3, White emerges with a Pawn
to the good and a far better position with 2 Q–B4, QxB
(else, White has an extra Bishop) 3 QxQ, PxQ; 4 BxB,
PxB; 5 RxP.

The Themes or Motifs

The elements of middle game tactics, as just considered, concentrate on the functioning of but a single
piece. But chess is a game with many pieces; and,
necessarily, as the elements of single pieces merge with
those of others, chessplay becomes more complex. The
resultant comminglings of elements are termed "combinations" or, more complex, "combined operations."

These operations, no matter how complex, are capable
of analysis into themes or motifs which can be learned
separately. Once the beginner knows these themes, he
can perceive their possibilities in any game and then
apply them. The possible combinations are myriad,
perhaps innumerable. But the themes or motifs from
which they are "combined" are not. And, like notes of
the scale or letters of the alphabet, they are building
blocks from which harmonies or words, the "combinations," can be formed.

Some of the combinations have already appeared in
the preceding pages. Most appear in the "Exercises in
Tactics" to follow (page 121). Here, however, are some
simpler examples of the combinational motifs (learn to
recognize each) and some of the principal "combined
operations."

The Pin. Most combinations depend on some form of a multiple (usually dual) attack. In the pin, this attack carries through on a straight line: rank, file, or diagonal. The principle is simple: a man is pinned against a more valuable man of the same side by the attacking piece. The pinned man cannot move without the valuable man being lost. And the pinned man, being immobilized, may either fail to function or may be held in place till force enough to capture it is assembled.

Illustration 90

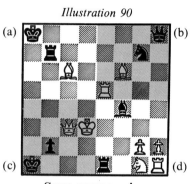

Some common pins

In each quadrant of illustration 90 is shown a common type of pin (take each quarter as a separate board): (a) an absolute pin: with the King behind the pin, the pin is "absolute," since it cannot be broken except by moving the King first. It is also a winning pin as a lesser piece assails the Rook; (b) a pin immobilizing the Knight: if on the move, Black can escape by moving his Queen; but, on the move, White can pile up on the Knight, by R–N5 or R–K7, and win it; (c) in this common endgame position, the White Queen holds the Black

Pawn from queening till 1 K–B2 effects its capture by the Queen and, incidentally, mate; (d) White's pinned Knight cannot escape except at the cost of . . . RxR; and 1 . . . B–K6 and 2 . . . RxN will win the Knight.

In illustration 91, a pin can be created which serves both defensively and to win. Though Black threatens to mate at QN7, White sets up the pin by 1 RxPch, K or QxR; 2 R–QB1. Then Black's Queen must fall, and White's passed Pawn candidate, his King Knight Pawn, ultimately goes on to queen on the Kingside.

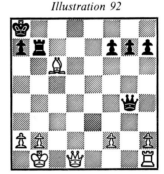

Illustration 91   *Illustration 92*

Creating a pin   **A simple counter attack**

Breaking a Pin. Any tactical motif can be met, given time (number of moves) and resources (the men to move). So it is with the pin. The absolute pin is the hardest to break—but even it can be broken, by moves or combinations which smite.

In illustration 92, White has an absolute pin and one which ensures a material gain on the move. The only way to break such a pin is by an immediate counter stroke. Here Black has 1 . . . Q–N3ch and 2 . . . QxB.

Illustration 93

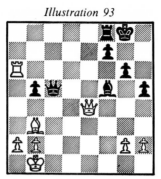

A more elaborate pin break

In illustration 93, White's Queen is in an absolute pin and apparently lost. But 1 RxPch (technically "destroying a guard," a motif presented later), BxR; 2 QxBch saves a draw for White, who can now check perpetually: 2 ... K–R1; 3 Q–R6ch, K–N1; 4 Q–N6ch, etc.

Note that tactical counter measures, particularly against a pin, must be violent moves: check or capture or mating threat or a counter combination. In the last example, White captured, sacrificing a Rook but destroying a guard, then checked by employing a counter pin.

The Fork. The double (or multiple) attack is inherent in the normal move of all chessmen, except in a sense the King. In the Knight and the Queen, with their eight-pronged moves, the fork—an attack in more than one direction at once—is almost commonplace. The Queen fork has appeared previously (page 96). The Rook and Bishop fork with difficulty: since they move in only two diverse directions, to fork at all deceptively they must catch two enemy men on a line perpendicular to their approach (see b and c, illustration 94). But the

Knight is a forker *par excellence:* its forking approach must be perceived from at least two moves away (more if it's made with the aid of a check or checks).

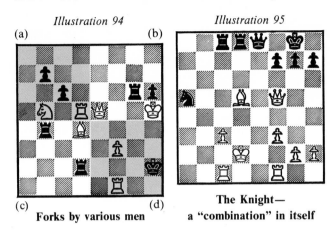

Illustration 94

(a)　　　　　　　(b)

(c)　　　　　　　(d)

Forks by various men

Illustration 95

**The Knight—
a "combination" in itself**

In illustration 94 (quadranted): (a) a Pawn forks Knight and Rook; (b) the Rook can fork King and Queen by 1 ... R–N4; (c) the Bishop forks two Rooks and wins at least the Exchange (minor piece for a Rook) by 1 B–B3; (d) even the King can fork on occasion, here by 1 ... K–N7.

In illustration 95, the Knight conducts a *tour de force,* ending with a "family fork." 1 ... N–N6ch wins an Exchange, but 1 ... N–B5ch wins even more: 2 K–Q1 (2 K–Q3, Q–K6ch; 3 K–B2, Q–K7ch leads to mate, as does 2 K–B2, Q–K7ch), N–K6ch is a family fork in which the Knight captures at will.

Setting up a Knight fork is a common tactical motif. And breaking a fork, as breaking a pin, requires violent counter-attacking methods.

Illustration 96   *Illustration 97*

Sacrificing,   **Breaking a fork**
a prelude to a fork

In illustration 96, Black extricates himself from a Rook fork by setting up a Knight fork which finally nets an Exchange: 1 ... QxR; 2 NxQ, N-K7ch etc.

In illustration 97, the disastrous-appearing fork can be countered. Not by the pin, 1 R-Q4, as 1 ... NxQ; 2 RxQ loses a whole Rook to 2 ... RxR. Not by the counter fork, as 1 N-K6 is futile against 1 ... BxN. But by a mating attack: 1 N-N6ch, PxN; 2 R-R4 mate.

Double Attack. The fork, as we have just seen, is an attack simultaneously on two separate targets which, by definition, is a combination. What is termed "Double Attack" in many chess texts is also basically a forking action but one characterized perhaps by being part of a continued operation.

In illustration 98, Black's winning combination starts with a simple Pawn attack, 1 ... P-QB4; 2 B-K3, setting the stage for the double attack. But not quite. For now 2 ... P-B5, though a double attack, can be countered by the mere trade of Queens: 3 QxQ, RxQ and 4 B-B2.

Illustration 98   *Illustration 99*

Combined elements   **A continued operation**

Instead, Black employs a *Zwischenzug* (an "in-between move"), 2 . . . QxQ; 3 RxQ, after which 3 . . . P–B5 effectively wins material.

In illustration 99, two double attacks evolve. If White has just played 1 B/KN3–Q6, attacking a Black Rook on KB1, he has attempted a "Masking Attack" aimed at winning the Pawn on his Q4, and Black has parried by 1 . . . R–B3 ready for 2 QxP? RxB. Now 2 B–K5 stages the first double attack, on Pawn and Rook, expecting 2 . . . NxB; 3 RxN with a favorable simplification of the position in view of his having an extra Pawn. The second double attack is the stinger which refutes the first: 2 . . . Q–Q4 carries a two-pronged threat: 3 . . . QxP mate and 3 . . . NxB. White must lose material to avoid the mate.

Discovered Attack. The Discovered Attack is quite different from the Double Attack as it involves attacks by two separate men; as one moves to attack it unmasks an attack by the other. As with all combinations, if a check figures in the action, the discovered attack is almost sure to be unrefutable.

Illustration 100   *Illustration 101*

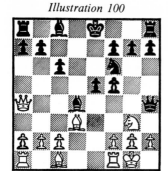 

There is no defense   **A defense is possible**

In illustration 100, Black uncovers an attack on White's Queen with 1 ... BxPch. As "a check must be respected," the Queen falls to 2 ... QxQ. This example is typical of a discovered attack combined with a check.

In illustration 101, three Black attempts at a discovered attack would be faulty. For there are checks possible in the action but, unfortunately, by White. Thus, 1 ... NxP, with attack of Knight on Rook and of Rook on Queen, would be met by 2 BxPch, and 2 ... KxB; 3 Q–B3ch, or 2 ... RxB; 3 Q–Q8ch, after which White captures the Knight. Likewise, the double-barreled Attack on the Queen by 1 ... N–B5 actually loses a Pawn to 2 BxPch, KxB; 3 Q–B3ch, N–K4; 4 RxN etc., or 2 ... RxB; 3 R–K8ch, R–N1; 4 Q–B3ch, etc. Similarly, 1 ... N–B6 is also met by 1 BxPch.

Checks are potent medicine either in reinforcing a combination or in breaking one.

Discovered Check. The form of discovered attack which involves a check by the man unmasked is termed "Discovered Check." It has the potency of the discovered attack with a check, plus also the fact that the man unmasked is usually further removed from the scene of action and so more likely itself to be immune from counter action.

Illustration 102

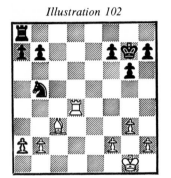

**The simple pattern
of a discovery**

Illustration 103

Setting up a discovery

In illustration 102, the essentials of a successful discovered check are presented. The Rook moves and unmasks a check by the Bishop, and the Rook has a fruitful target, as seen on 1 ... R–Q8 dis. ch. Though Black has all the three recourses for getting out of check (moving the King, interposing a man, and capturing the checking man), even the latter costs him materially: 1 ... NxB; 2 RxR.

In illustration 103, Black has the ingredients of a discovered attack, and the Rook to be unmasked is secure against attack. But Black has no target for the unmasking Bishop. So, to stage a profitable discovery, he assails White's Knight by 1 ... P–QN4. Now, on any

Knight move, it falls: 2 N–B5, BxN dis. ch or 2 N–B3, B–Q5 dis. ch followed by ... R or BxN. White can try one defense: 2 R–B3, hoping for 2 ... RxR; 3 NxR; but 2 ... R–R7, instead, leaves both Knight and Rook in jeopardy as the threat of discovery still holds.

Double Check. There are checks and checks. On a simple check, the side under fire has three ways of evading the check: moving the King, interposing a man, or capturing the checking man. Part of the potency of a Knight is that the side in check by a Knight has only two recourses, moving the King or capturing the Knight: it is impossible to interpose. The Double Check allows of but one kind of reply: moving the King. Hence, it is the most potent check and a more vigorous form of a discovered check.

Illustration 104

A typical pattern

Illustration 105

Preparing a finale

In illustration 104, though White has all his pieces *en prise,* and mate threatening, 1 B–B6 dbl. ch wins outright. On either the Rook check or the Bishop's, Black could capture the checking piece, interpose one of his own, or move his King. Here he can only move the King, and 2 R–R8 mate follows.

In illustration 105, the power of a potential double check is such that the ultimate in a violent finish is indicated. Black mates after 1 ... QxBch; 2 KxQ, R–B6 dbl. ch. Neither capture of either checking piece avails, nor any interposition, and 3 K–N1, R–B8 mate is forced.

The X-ray Attack. This attack has been also called the "Skewer," a more homely name but perhaps equally appropriate. Like the pin, the X-ray Attack catches two men on the same line, but with the more valuable in front of the other. In consequence, provided the attacking piece is both protected and less valuable, the valuable enemy piece has to step aside and the attack penetrates through the square on which it stood and catches the man behind.

Illustration 106

The typical pattern

In illustration 106, a typical X-ray attack is in operation. Black's King has no choice but to step aside, and the Rook falls.

Illustration 107

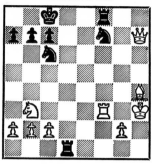

Installing an X-ray

Usually, of course, some preparation is necessary to set up the X-ray. In illustration 107, Black forces matters with a family fork, 1 ... N-N4ch, and is promptly repaid for his sacrifice by 2 BxN, R-R8ch, winning White's Queen.

Interference. The process of "Interference" derives probably from problem composing, which has produced brilliant examples. It is essentially a matter of throwing

Illustration 108

A simple pattern

a monkey wrench into the opponent's line of communications.

In illustration 108, Black, though behind a full piece, would win if ... QxP mate were possible. Under the circumstances, a violent sacrifice is justified, and 1 ... R–Q6 sets up a classic form of interference. 2 QxR loses the Queen, but either 2 NxR or 2 BxR permits the mate.

Illustration 109

Preparing for an interference

In illustration 109, White has pinned Black's King Bishop, which is protected by Queen and King. As each is adjacent to the Bishop, Black has no lines of communication to be cut, and White cannot insert an interference. By relying on other tactics, however, White separates Black's Queen and Bishop. 1 B–KB4 drives the Queen. Now 1 ... QxB constitutes a "Removal of the Guard" (see next section), allowing 2 QxB mate. And 1 ... Q–B3 permits an X-ray attack which wins the Black Bishop: 2 B–KN5, Q–Q3; 3 BxB. So Black must play 1 ... Q–B4 or ... Q–N5. Now there is a line of communication, and White cuts it with 2 P–Q6 and wins the Black King Bishop, and more.

Removing a Guard. This process is akin to interference in that essentially it also severs communications. It does so by deflecting a protecting man.

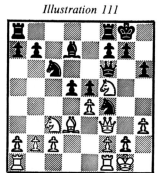

Illustration 110   *Illustration 111*

The essential pattern   The pattern elaborated

Illustration 110 represents the essentials of a Removal. By 1 BxP, White takes off the Pawn with impunity; for 1 ... PxB deprives Black's Knight of its support, and 2 RxN gives White an ending which can be won by precise play.

In the illustration 111, White's Knight on KB5 seems well supported, by Pawn and Bishop. But 1 ... PxP cuts down one guard, and either 2 NxKP or 2 BxP leaves that Knight insufficiently guarded. 2 QxP maintains two protectors for the Knight; but, by a second removal, 2 ... NxB, Black so weakens the guard that 3 ... QxN or 3 BxN is possible.

The Overburdened Man. This pattern for combinations is so much like that of Removing a Guard that the first diagram illustrating the latter (illustration 110) also serves for this. There Black's Queen Knight Pawn is the overburdened man. It cannot support both the Knight and the Queen Rook Pawn. The technique for exploiting an overburdened man is also much the same, the removal of a guard. The combinational element enters only if a temporary sacrifice is required. And the principal difficulty for the attacker is to perceive that there is an overburdened man in the position.

Illustration 112

An object lesson

In illustration 112, White's Queen is working like a Trojan, a fact which ought to alert Black. Of course, the Queen is centrally placed and so commands a great many squares. But is that all there is to be said? 1 ... PxP; 2 QxP seems to gain Black nothing, and everything else seems well protected. Inspection, however, reveals that the Queen is not only protecting men but also the square QB1. There is Black's clue, and 1 ... RxP wins, drastically. For the Queen can go nowhere and still safely prevent 2 ... Q-B8 mate; and 2 N-B2, RxN; 3 R-K2, RxR; 4 Q-Q1 (still protecting QB1), Q-B6ch is Black's relentless march to a mate.

(a) *Illustration 113* (b)

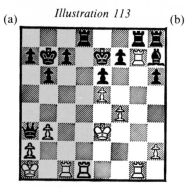

Deceptive burdens

In illustration 113, two quite deceptive instances of overburdened men exist (treat each half-diagram as separate, with other men not affecting the play on the other half). In (a), 1 ... R–Q7 constitutes a mating threat if only 2 RxR were impossible. With that very thought, it becomes apparent that the Rook on Q1 is overburdened: 1 ... R–Q7!; 2 RxR, QxR is mate. In (b), Black's pieces are all solidly protected, seemingly. But the temporary sacrifice, 1 RxB, reveals Black's weakness. He has lost a piece as either ... RxR is countered by 2 RxR.

The main lesson to be gained from the overburdened man—well worth the extra section devoted to it—is that, on defense, a player must not strive too much for economy. It is all very well, and good chess, to put each man to work, double work if possible, positionally and especially on the attack. But, on the defense, for one man to guard two attacked men, or squares, is actually to leave one or the other unguarded.

The Dead End. This combinational motif is, like the Overburdened Man, usually, if not always, a result of poor play by the defender. It could well be called "The Trap," except that term has come to have a broader meaning in chess. Indeed, a typical example of the Dead End is named the "Noah's Ark" trap, because it is supposedly so venerable.

Illustration 114   *Illustration 115*

The Noah's Ark   **Another engulfable piece**

Illustration 114 epitomizes the Dead End. White has erred in ensconcing his Bishop whence it has no retreat. If Black is alert, he plays 1 ... PxP, and White has nothing better than the dubious 2 B-Q5. For 2 NxQP runs him headlong into the Noah's Ark trap: 2 ... NxN; 3 QxN, P-B4; 4 Q-Q1, P-B5 in which his King Bishop is trapped.

Bishops are peculiarly susceptible to Pawn entrapments; and, in illustration 115, White has been careless. He ought not to have played P-K3 or P-KN3, or at least ought to have swapped his Queen Bishop for Black's Knight. For Black now has: 1 ... N-K5; 2 Q-B2,

P-KB3; 3 B-R4 or B-B4, P-N4, winning a piece.

Sometimes, the cul de sac is not absolute; it may be that the exit is just inadequate for the number of pieces which need it (see illustration 116). Or, there may be a Dead End on a wide-open board (illustration 117).

Illustration 116

A traffic jam

1 P-R4 precipitates a crisis for Black; for 1 ... N-R2, to save the Knight, closes off retreat for his Bishop vs. 2 P-KN4 and 3 P-R5.

Illustration 117

A choked freeway

Black has cleverly won a Pawn, but now ruefully runs into 1 P-QR4, N-R6; 2 B-K7, N-N8; 3 K-B2, a dead end for the Knight on a nearly empty board.

The Back Rank Mate. Of mating attacks, there is literally no end, and it is impossible to give all kinds here. But the mate on the back rank, or threat of it, figures in the winning of so many games that the beginner must be thoroughly aware of it. It unfortunately befalls that very student who most faithfully observes the rule to safely castle and wisely retain the Pawn barrier before his King. In its simpler form, it commonly costs a piece (as in illustration 118). But it figured also as an important element in the finish of Morphy's Immortal Game (illustration 119): 13 RxN, RxR; 14 R-Q1, Q-K3; 15 BxRch, NxB; 16 Q-N8ch, NxQ; 17 R-Q8 mate!

Illustration 118

A scatheless capture

White plays 1 NxB with impunity as 1 . . . RxN brings on 2 R-K8 mate. Often a piece is thus left "hanging" by the illusory protection of a guardian of the back rank.

Illustration 119

Morphy's immortal finish

Morphy's play utilized some pins, and, at the end, exploited the overburdened state of Black's Knight, which had to guard QN1 and also blockade the Queen file against the Back Rank Mate.

Tactical Checkmates

The mate on the back rank is not the only common mate, of course. But, in the space available, only a few even of the tactical (surprise) mates can be shown. In general, the advice to beginners against being mated is: eye jealously any enemy man which strikes at the King field—the square on which the King stands and those adjacent. Or, indeed, any man which can come anywhere near one's King.

Quiz on Tactical Checkmates

Solutions on page 159.

The following positions have all been set (for convenience) with White to move and mate (not that Black cannot mate on occasion). With a proper knowledge of how the men move, and the notice that White does mate, you should be able to perceive the point and method of each mating combination.

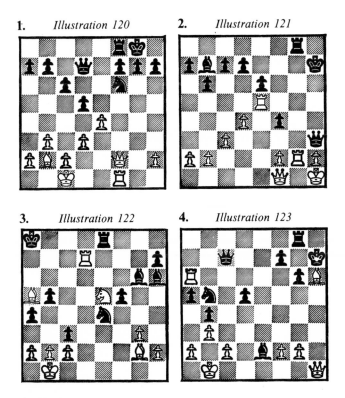

1.   *Illustration 120*   **2.**   *Illustration 121*

3.   *Illustration 122*   **4.**   *Illustration 123*

5. *Illustration 124*   **6.** *Illustration 125*

7. *Illustration 126*   **8.** *Illustration 127*

9. *Illustration 128*   **10.** *Illustration 129*

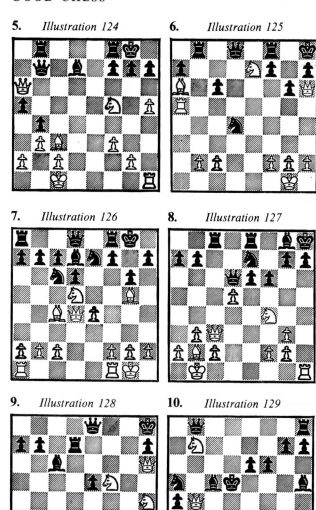

11. *Illustration 130* **12.** *Illustration 131*

 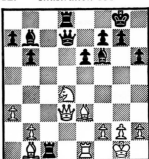

Exercises in Tactics (A Quiz)

Solutions on page 159.

The following exercises will launch the learner into the welter of tactical legerdemain.

Illustration 132 *Illustration 133*

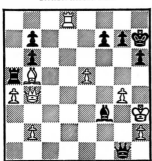 

1. How does White win? **2. Can White win? How?**

Illustration 134

3. Is 1 R-KR5 playable?

Illustration 135

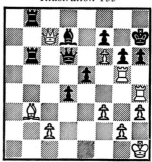

4. Aside from 1 QxQ, what?

Illustration 136

5. After the check, what wins?

Illustration 137

6. Can White mate here?

Illustration 138

7. Or here?

Illustration 139

8. What wins?

Illustration 140

Illustration 141

9. Again, White mates. How? **10. White wins a Pawn. How?**

Illustration 142

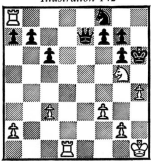

Illustration 143

11. What wins for White? **12. What mates for White?**

Illustration 144

Illustration 145

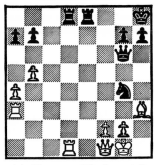

13. Black's turn—what wins? **14. How can Black mate?**

Illustration 146

15. Can Black mate? How?

Illustration 147

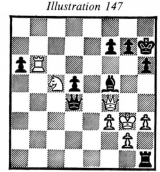

16. And here?

Illustration 148

17. How does Black win?

Illustration 149

18. How does Black mate?

Illustration 150

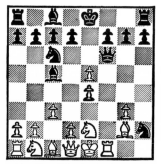

19. Can Black win? How?

Illustration 151

20. And here?

Illustration 152

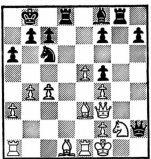

21. How can Black mate?

Illustration 153

22. And here?

Illustration 154

23. Set up a Black mate?

Illustration 155

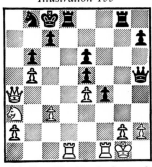

24. See Black's dual mate?

Part IV
Chess Movies

Chess Movie I
Tricks, Traps, and Stratagems

"Beware the sleazy trap" is the judgment of the Book of Aphorisms. Time misspent on a spurious goal is time wasted. It does not follow, however, that a trap—a baited combination—is bad. The trap which follows was actually played by two American "invincibles," Bobby Fischer, an eight-time U.S. champion, and Sammy Reshevsky, a six-time U.S. champion. This Sicilian Defense begins with 1 P–K4, P–QB4; 2 N–KB3, N–QB3 (see illustration 156).

Illustration 156

Illustration 157

The game follows the orthodox line: 3 P–Q4, PxP; 4 NxP, P–KN3—a wing development of the Bishop called fianchettoing the Bishop. In conjunction with the open Queen Bishop file, the Bishop will exert pressure through the center (see illustration 157).

Now the game follows a natural bent: 5 N–QB3, B–N2; 6 B–K3, N–B3. White's objective is to control the center with his men and Black aims to balance. Little does Black realize the implicit dangers of the position. And he lulls himself into a false sense of security (see illustration 158).

Illustration 158	*Illustration 159*
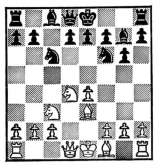	

With 7 B–QB4, White anticipates things to come. 7 ...0–0; 8 B–N3, N–QR4 follow. Black's last is bad. 9 P–K5, N–K1; 10 BxPch ruins Black's position. He resigns (see illustration 159).

On 10 ... RxB; 11 N–K6, White wins the Queen. On 10 ... KxB, N–K6, KxN, or K–R1; 11 Q–Q5ch, the King is soon mated.

CHESS MOVIE II
Double Fianchetto, Double Trouble

Less than a century ago, the development of the Bishop on the wing, or flank, called the fianchetto of the Bishop, was frowned upon. The immediate occupation and control of the center was mod, and it received the nod of the classicists. With the advent of hypermodernism, which incorporated belief in wing control of the center, the fianchettoes became popular. So the King's fianchetto, the Queen's fianchetto, and the double fianchetto became fashionable.

The pattern is set from the game Benko-Horowitz, after 1 P-QB4, P-QB3; 2 N-KB3, P-Q4; 3 P-QN3, N-B3; 4 P-N3, P-K3; 5 B-KN2, B-K2 (reaching illustration 160).

Illustration 160   *Illustration 161*

Light skirmishing is the order of the play. White reveals that he banks on the double fianchetto. And Black chooses a usual deployment, without committing himself. White's Bishops are directed straight at the center, where Black is vulnerable. There follows: 6 0–0, 0–0; 7 B–N2, P–QR4; 8 P–QR3, P–B4; 9 PxP, PxP; 10 P–Q4, N–R3 (see illustration 161).

In the center, White is supreme. On Black's right flank, the second player has pinpointed a weakness. And he is ready to exploit it. There follows: 11 N–B3, B–B4; 12 N–K5, PxP; 13 QxP, N–B4; 14 NxQP, NxP; 15 Q–KB4, NxN (see illustration 162).

Illustration 162   *Illustration 163*

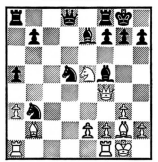   

For a moment, it seems Black is in the lead. He must gain what is technically known as the Exchange—a Rook for a Knight. Usually this is decisive. But not here. There follows: 16 QxB, NxR; 17 NxP, Q–B1; 18 N–R6ch, K–R1; 19 QxN, N–B7; 20 Q–N8ch, Resigns (see illustration 163).

To a neophyte, White has erred; he has parted with his Queen. To a sophisticate, it is an entirely different story. White has enjoyed springing a trap which is known as Philidor's Legacy, named after the ancient grandmaster. The sting is 20 ... RxQ; 21 N–B7 mate.

Chess Movie III
Out of Mate

"What is good enough for my opponent is good enough for me," may be perfect philosophy if your opponent is a Capablanca. But it would not win for you if you were across the board from the grandmaster. Nor will it do if you are merely emulating without comprehending. In this Vienna Opening—Horowitz vs. Anonymous—from a simultaneous exhibition, Black imitates White. But White quickly forecloses the possibility: The game begins with 1 P-K4, P-K4; 2 N-QB3, N-QB3; 3 B-B4, B-B4 (see illustration 164).

Illustration 164   *Illustration 165*

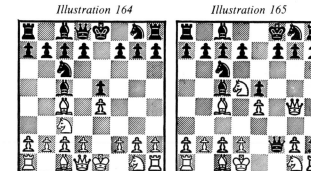

Black follows in White's tack. Now White plays 4 Q-N4, and that ends Black's copycatting. So Black plays 4 ... Q-B3, apparently threatening mate! White plays 5 N-Q5. Black continues 5 ... QxP mate. And White replies 6 K-Q1, *out of mate.* So Black defends his King Knight Pawn with 6 ... K-B1 (see illustration 165).

Now 7 N–R3 prods the Queen, and 7 ... Q–Q5 is forced. 8 P–Q3 is an attempt to snare the Queen, and 8 ... B–N3 is to create an escape square. Then White takes a bead on the enemy King with 9 R–B1, and Black counters with 9 ... N–B3. White's Queen is attacked (see illustration 166).

Illustration 166

Illustration 167

10 RxN is the move to counter that attack, and Black parries with 10 ... P–Q3, again attacking White's Queen. But here comes the surprise: 11 QxPch. Black did not dream White would part with his Queen. Of course, Black plays 11 ... KxQ, and there follows 12 B–R6ch, K–N1 (see illustration 167).

This panel reveals White's plan. There follows 13 R–N6ch, and Black is forced to capture. Black plays 13 ... RPxR and 14 N–B6 mate spells *finis. Sacrificio benevolente con amore* is the inimitable spirit of this game.

CHESS MOVIE IV
Mate at Eight

The asymmetrical Sicilian Defense, a double-edged struggle, leads to piquant play. White often preempts the Kingside, Black, the opposite wing, and delayed action occurs in the center. Here White early takes a critical central initiative.

This game is from a simultaneous exhibition about 1935 between Horowitz (White) vs. Carrigan. It begins with 1 P-K4, P-QB4; 2 N-KB3, P-Q3; 3 P-Q4, PxP; 4 NxP, N-KB3; 5 N-QB3, P-KN3 (see illustration 168).

Illustration 168

Illustration 169

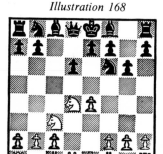

Then follow moves typical of this pattern: 6 P-B4, B-N2; 7 P-K5, PxP; 8 PxP, N-Q4; 9 B-N5ch, K-B1. Black's King moves, and Black forfeits the privilege of castling—a demerit for Black. Black's King is now a fixed target and White conjures up ways to waylay the monarch (see illustration 169).

The game continues with 10 0-0 and with 10 ... BxP,

Black grabs a Pawn. So White promotes his development with 11 B–R6ch, and 11 ... K–N1; 12 NxN, QxN follows. Black has gained a puny Pawn. But his King "must suffer the slings and arrows of outrageous fortune." Predatory loot must always be viewed with suspicion (see illustration 170).

Illustration 170   *Illustration 171*

With 13 N–B5 White issues a challenge. And Black must be careful. A misstep will cost his Queen. He plays 13 ... Q–B4ch; and there follows: 14 K–R1, Q–B2; 15 B–QB4, BxN; 16 RxB, B–B3 (see illustration 171).

Illustration 172

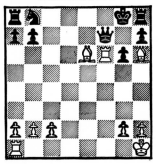

White announces mate: 17 Q–Q5! P–K3 (forced); 18 QxKP, PxQ; 19 BxPch, Q–B2; 20 RxB! and mate follows (see illustration 172). What a picture. There is simply no way for Black, nearly a Queen up, to avoid mate.

Part V
Model Games

The following tale is told of two surly grandmasters, Alexander Alekhine, chess champion of the world, and his confrere and challenger, Evfim Bogolubov, mighty paladins who had been feuding. During a conviviality, Alekhine was called upon for a speech.

"Last night I dreamed that I had died," he began, "and as all good chessplayers do, I made for heaven. As I reached the portals, the resonant voice of St. Peter questioned, 'Who is there?' Meekly, I replied, 'It is I, Alexander Alekhine, chess champion of the world.'

"'Sorry,' was the rejoinder, 'we do not accept chessplayers in heaven.' Dejected, I was about to go. But before leaving the pearly gates, I took a quick look around. And whom did I spy? None other than my good friend Bogolubov.

"'Why, there is Bogolubov,' I stammered. 'Is he not a chessplayer?'

"'No, indeed not,' said St. Peter. 'He only thinks he is a chessplayer.'"

All of which leads to the chessplayer and further—to chess itself. What *is* chess? Is it a science or an art? Is it a puzzle to be unraveled in solitude or a game in the ordinary sense?

Chess is a fight, a struggle between two minds, a contest in which the mimic battlefield is the chessboard. And over this arena are employed weapons, tangible and intangible—Knights, Bishops, Rooks, and Queens; psychological overtones; the blending of talent and knowledge and nerve; traps, pitfalls, and swindles; *fingerfehlers* and mental slips.

To play chess is a matter of half an hour. To play it well is the matter of a lifetime.

There is no better way to learn to play than to play. Doing *is* learning.

In the following section are games culled from important tournaments and matches of the past and present—presented, purposely, without analytical comment. These depict whole games: openings, middle games, and endings. The reader would do well to play out these games by the masters himself; in the process he is sure to pick up invaluable ideas and lessons.

GIUOCO PIANO			13 NxQ	....
Warsaw, 1844			*Illustration 173*	

Illustration 173

HOFFMAN	PETROFF
WHITE	BLACK
1 P-K4	P-K4
2 N-KB3	N-QB3
3 B-B4	B-B4
4 P-B3	N-B3
5 P-Q4	PxP
6 P-K5	N-K5
7 B-Q5	NxKBP
8 KxN	PxPch
9 K-N3	PxP
10 BxP	N-K2
11 N-N5	NxB
12 NxBP	O-O

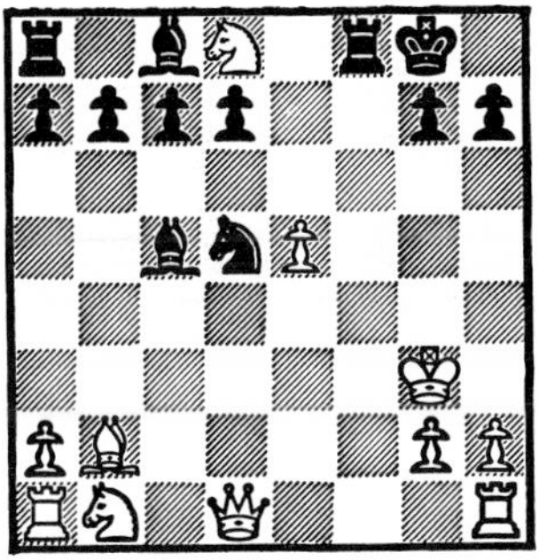

13	B-B7ch
14 K-R3	P-Q3ch
15 P-K6	N-B5ch
16 K-N4	NxKP
17 P-N3	NxNch

18	K-N5	R-B4ch
19	K-N4	R-B3ch
20	K-R4	R-B5ch
21	K-N5	N-K3ch
22	K-R5	P-N3ch
23	K-R6	R-R5ch
24	PxR	B-K6 mate

RUY LOPEZ
Breslau, 1859

ANDERSSEN	LANGE
WHITE	BLACK
1 P-K4	P-K4
2 N-KB3	N-QB3
3 B-N5	N-Q5
4 NxN	PxN
5 B-B4	N-B3
6 P-K5	P-Q4
7 B-N3	B-KN5
8 P-KB3	N-K5
9 0-0	P-Q6
10 PxB	B-B4ch
11 K-R1	N-N6ch
12 PxN	Q-N4
13 R-B5	....

(See illustration 174)

13	P-KR4
14 NPxP	QxR
15 P-N4	RxPch
16 PxR	Q-K5
17 Q-B3	Q-R5ch

Illustration 174

Position after 13 R–B5

| 18 Q-R3 | Q-K8ch |
| **Resigns** | |

QUEEN'S GAMBIT DECLINED
St. Petersburg, 1896

PILLSBURY	EM. LASKER
WHITE	BLACK
1 P-Q4	P-Q4
2 P-QB4	P-K3
3 N-QB3	N-KB3
4 N-B3	P-B4
5 B-N5	BPxP
6 QxP	N-B3
7 Q-R4	B-K2
8 0-0-0	Q-R4
9 P-K3	B-Q2
10 K-N1	P-KR3
11 PxP	PxP

12	N-Q4	0-0
13	BxN	BxB
14	Q-R5	NxN
15	PxN	B-K3
16	P-B4	QR-B1
17	P-B5	RxN
18	PxB	R-QR6
19	PxPch	RxP
20	PxR	Q-N3ch
21	B-N5	QxBch
22	K-R1	R-B2
23	R-Q2	R-B5
24	KR-Q1	R-B6
25	Q-B5	Q-B5
26	K-N2	RxP

Illustration 175

27	Q-K6ch	K-R2
28	KxR	Q-B6ch
29	K-R4	P-N4ch
30	KxP	Q-B5ch
31	K-R5	B-Q1ch
32	Q-N6	PxQ mate

QUEEN'S GAMBIT ACCEPTED

London, 1834

	DE LABOUR-DONNAIS	MAC-DONNELL
	WHITE	BLACK
1	P-Q4	P-Q4
2	P-QB4	PxP
3	P-K3	P-K4
4	BxP	PxP
5	PxP	N-KB3
6	N-QB3	B-K2
7	N-B3	0-0
8	B-K3	P-B3
9	P-KR3	QN-Q2
10	B-N3	N-N3
11	0-0	KN-Q4
12	P-QR4	P-QR4
13	N-K5	B-K3
14	B-B2	P-KB4
15	Q-K2	P-B5
16	B-Q2	Q-K1
17	QR-K1	B-B2
18	Q-K4	P-N3

(See illustration 176)

19	BxP	NxB
20	QxN	B-B5
21	Q-R6	BxR
22	BxP	PxB
23	NxNP	N-B1
24	Q-R8ch	K-B2
25	Q-R7ch	K-B3

Illustration 176

Position after 18 ... P–N3

26	N–B4	B–Q6
27	R–K6ch	K–N4
28	Q–R6ch	K–B4
29	P–N4 mate	

GIUOCO PIANO
London, 1845

Horwitz	Staunton
WHITE	BLACK
1 P–K4	P–K4
2 N–KB3	N–QB3
3 B–B4	B–B4
4 P–B3	N–B3
5 P–Q3	P–Q4
6 PxP	NxP
7 P–QN4	B–N3
8 P–N5	QN–K2
9 NxP	0–0
10 B–N2	B–K3

11	0–0	K–R1
12	P–QR4	P–KB3
13	N–B3	N–N3
14	B–R3	R–K1
15	Q–N3	N/3–B5
16	R–R2	P–QR3
17	PxP	PxP
18	B–B1	QR–N1

Illustration 177

19	Q–B2	B–N5
20	B/4xN	N–K7ch
21	K–R1	QxB
22	P–B4	QxN
23	P–R3	BxBP
24	N–Q2	N–N6ch
25	K–R2	Q–B5
26	RxB	N–B8ch
27	K–N1	Q–R7ch
28	KxN	Q–R8 mate

VIENNA OPENING
Vienna, 1859

HAMPE   STEINITZ

WHITE   BLACK

1	P-K4	P-K4
2	N-QB3	N-KB3
3	P-B4	P-Q4
4	KPxP	NxP
5	PxP	NxN
6	NPxN	Q-R5ch
7	K-K2	B-N5ch
8	N-B3	N-B3
9	P-Q4	0-0-0
10	B-Q2	BxNch
11	PxB	NxP
12	PxN	B-B4

Illustration 178

13	Q-K1	Q-B5ch
14	K-Q1	QxBP
15	QR-N1	QxKBPch
16	Q-K2	RxBch

17	KxR	R-Q1ch
18	K-B1	B-R6ch
19	R-N2	Q-B6
20	B-R3ch	K-N1
21	Q-N5	Q-Q7ch
22	K-N1	Q-Q8ch
23	RxQ	RxR mate

SICILIAN DEFENSE
Paris, 1858

MORPHY   ANDERSSEN

WHITE   BLACK

1	P-K4	P-QB4
2	P-Q4	PxP
3	N-KB3	N-QB3
4	NxP	P-K3
5	N-N5	P-Q3
6	B-KB4	P-K4
7	B-K3	P-B4
8	QN-B3	P-B5

Illustration 179

9	N-Q5	PxB
10	N/N-B7ch	K-B2
11	Q-B3ch	N-B3
12	B-B4	N-Q5
13	NxNch	P-Q4
14	BxPch	K-N3
15	Q-R5ch	KxN
16	PxP	NxPch
17	K-K2	Resigns

FOUR KNIGHTS'
GAME
New York, 1857

PAULSEN	MORPHY
WHITE	BLACK
1 P-K4	P-K4
2 N-KB3	N-QB3
3 N-B3	N-B3
4 B-N5	B-B4
5 0-0	0-0
6 NxP	R-K1
7 NxN	QPxN
8 B-B4	P-QN4
9 B-K2	NxP
10 NxN	RxN
11 B-B3	R-K3
12 P-B3	Q-Q6
13 P-QN4	B-N3
14 P-QR4	PxP
15 QxP	B-Q2
16 R-R2	QR-K1

17	Q-R6	....

Illustration 180

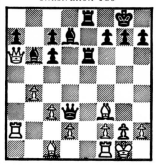

17	....	QxB
18	PxQ	R-N3ch
19	K-R1	B-R6
20	R-Q1	B-N7ch
21	K-N1	QBxPch
22	K-B1	B-N7ch
23	K-N1	B-R6ch
24	K-R1	BxP
25	Q-B1	BxQ
26	RxB	R-K7
27	R-R1	R-R3
28	P-Q4	B-K6
	Resigns	

VIENNA GAME
London, 1899

STEINETZ	EM. LASKER
WHITE	BLACK
1 P-K4	P-K4
2 N-QB3	N-KB3
3 P-B4	P-Q4
4 P-Q3	N-B3
5 BPxP	QNxP
6 P-Q4	N-N3
7 PxP	NxP
8 NxN	QxN
9 N-B3	B-N5
10 B-K2	0-0-0
11 P-B3	B-Q3
12 0-0	KR-K1
13 P-KR3	B-Q2
14 N-N5	N-R5

Illustration 181

| 15 N-B3 | NxP |
| 16 KxN | BxPch |

17 K-B2	P-KB3
18 R-KN1	P-KN4
19 BxP	PxB
20 RxP	Q-K3
21 Q-Q3	B-B5
22 R-R1	BxR
23 NxB	Q-B3ch
24 B-B3	B-B4
25 NxP	Q-KN3
26 Q-N5	P-B3
27 Q-R5	R-K2
28 R-R5	B-N5
29 R-KN5	Q-B7ch
30 K-N3	BxB
	Resigns

EVANS' GAMBIT
St. Petersburg, 1895

TCHIGORIN	EM. LASKER
WHITE	BLACK
1 P-K4	P-K4
2 N-KB3	N-QB3
3 B-B4	B-B4
4 P-QN4	BxP
5 P-B3	B-B4
6 0-0	P-Q3
7 P-Q4	B-N3
8 P-QR4	N-B3
9 B-QN5	P-QR3
10 BxNch	PxB
11 P-R5	B-R2

12	PxP	NxP
13	Q-K2	P-Q4
14	N-Q4	NxQBP
15	NxN	BxN
16	Q-Q3	P-QB4

Illustration 182

17	Q-N3	B-K3
18	B-N5	Q-Q2
19	QR-B1	P-KB3
20	PxP	PxP
21	B-B4	KR-N1
22	Q-B3	0-0-0
23	KR-K1	P-B5
24	Q-K2	B-KB4
25	Q-R2	RxPch
26	K-R1	RxP
	Resigns	

RUY LOPEZ
New York, 1918

CAPABLANCA   FONAROFF

	WHITE	BLACK
1	P-K4	P-K4
2	N-KB3	N-QB3
3	B-N5	N-B3
4	0-0	P-Q3
5	P-Q4	B-Q2
6	N-B3	B-K2
7	R-K1	PxP
8	NxP	NxN
9	QxN	BxB
10	NxB	0-0
11	Q-B3	P-B3
12	N-Q4	N-Q2
13	N-B5	B-B3
14	Q-KN3	N-K4
15	B-B4	Q-B2
16	QR-Q1	QR-Q1

Illustration 183

17	RxP	RxR
18	BxN	R-Q8
19	RxR	BxB
20	N-R6ch	K-R1
21	QxB	QxQ'
22	NxPch	**Resigns**

NIMZO-INDIAN
DEFENSE
New York, 1944

DENKER	FINE
WHITE	BLACK
1 P-Q4	N-KB3
2 P-QB4	P-K3
3 N-QB3	B-N5
4 P-K3	P-QN3
5 B-Q3	B-N2
6 N-B3	N-K5
7 0-0	NxN
8 PxN	BxP
9 R-N1	B-R4
10 B-R3	P-Q3
11 P-B5	0-0
12 PxQP	PxP
13 P-K4	R-K1
14 P-K5	PxP
15 NxP	Q-N4
16 P-N3	P-N3
17 Q-R4	Q-Q1
18 KR-B1	P-QN4
19 BxQNP	Q-Q4

20	P-B3	B-N3

Illustration 184

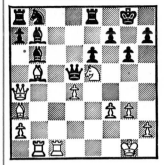

21	R-B5	BxR
22	BxB	R-KB1
23	B-B4	B-B3
24	BxQ	BxQ
25	BxQR	**Resigns**

QUEEN'S GAMBIT
DECLINED
Cambridge Springs, 1904

PILLSBURY	LASKER
WHITE	BLACK
1 P-Q4	P-Q4
2 P-QB4	P-K3
3 N-QB3	N-KB3
4 N-B3	P-B4
5 B-N5	PxQP
6 QxP	N-B3
7 BxN	PxB

8	Q-R4	PxP
9	R-Q1	B-Q2
10	P-K3	N-K4
11	NxN	PxN
12	QxBP	Q-N3
13	B-K2	QxNP
14	0-0	R-B1
15	Q-Q3	R-B2
16	N-K4	B-K2
17	N-Q6ch	K-B1
18	N-B4	Q-N4
19	P-B4	PxP
20	Q-Q4	P-B3
21	QxP/B	Q-QB4
22	N-K5	B-K1
23	N-N4	P-B4
24	Q-R6ch	K-B2
25	B-B4	R-B3

Illustration 185

26	RxPch	QxR
27	R-KB1	QxRch
28	KxQ	B-Q2

29	Q-R5ch	K-N1
30	N-K5	Resigns

QUEEN'S GAMBIT
ACCEPTED
Nuremberg, 1906

MARSHALL   WOLF

WHITE   BLACK

1	P-Q4	P-Q4
2	P-QB4	PxP
3	N-KB3	N-KB3
4	N-B3	P-QR3
5	P-K3	P-K3
6	BxP	P-B4
7	0-0	N-B3
8	P-QR3	Q-B2
9	Q-K2	P-QN4
10	B-R2	B-N2
11	PxP	BxP
12	P-QN4	B-Q3
13	B-N2	0-0
14	QR-B1	QR-Q1
15	B-N1	B-R1
16	N-K4	N-Q4

(See illustration 186)

17	N/4-N5	P-N3
18	NxRP	KxN
19	N-N5ch	K-N1
20	Q-R5	P-B3
21	BxNP	R-Q2
22	NxP	R-R2

Illustration 186

Position after 16 ... N–Q4

23	BxRch	QxB
24	QxQch	KxQ
25	NxRch	BxN
26	KR–Q1	N/3–K2
27	P–K4	N–QN3
28	R–B7	K–N1
29	BxP	N–N3
30	R–Q8	**Resigns**

FRENCH DEFENSE

Boston, 1944

	RESHEVSKY	VASCON-CELLOS
	WHITE	BLACK
1	P–K4	P–K3
2	P–Q4	P–Q4
3	P–K5	P–QB4
4	PxP	N–Q2
5	N–KB3	BxP

6	B–Q3	N–K2
7	0–0	N–QB3
8	B–KB4	Q–B2
9	N–B3	P–QR3
10	R–K1	Q–N3
11	B–N3	QxP
12	NxP	PxN
13	R–N1	Q–R6
14	P–K6	N–B3
15	PxPch	KxP
16	B–R4	N–QN5
17	N–K5ch	K–B1
18	BxN	NxB
19	BxPch	KxB
20	RxPch	B–K2
21	Q–R5	R–B1
22	Q–N5ch	K–R1

Illustration 187

23	N–N6ch	PxN
24	Q–R6ch	K–N1
25	QxPch	K–R1
26	R/7xB	**Resigns**

OLD INDIAN DEFENSE
Copenhagen, 1960

	PETROSIAN	LARSEN
	WHITE	BLACK
1	P-Q4	N-KB3
2	P-QB4	P-Q3
3	N-KB3	B-N5
4	N-B3	QN-Q2
5	P-K4	P-K4
6	B-K2	B-K2
7	O-O	O-O
8	B-K3	B-R4
9	N-Q2	BxB
10	QxB	PxP
11	BxP	R-K1
12	P-B4	B-B1
13	QR-Q1	P-QR3
14	Q-B3	P-B3
15	P-KN4	N-B4
16	BxQN	PxB
17	P-K5	N-Q2
18	N/2-K4	Q-B2
19	R-Q3	N-N3
20	P-N3	QR-Q1
21	KR-Q1	B-K2
22	P-N5	N-B1
23	Q-R5	RxR
24	RxR	R-Q1

(See illustration 188)

25	N-B6ch	PxN

Illustration 188

Position after 24 ... R-Q1

26	R-R3	K-B1
27	QxP	K-K1
28	P-N6	B-B1
29	P-N7	BxP
30	QxB	Q-K2
31	N-K4	R-Q8ch
32	K-B2	P-B4
33	N-B6ch	K-Q1
34	R-R8ch	Resigns

GRUENFELD DEFENSE
New York, 1956

	D. BYRNE	FISCHER
	WHITE	BLACK
1	N-KB3	N-KB3
2	P-B4	P-KN3
3	N-B3	B-N2
4	P-Q4	O-O

5	B-B4	P-Q4
6	Q-N3	PxP
7	QxBP	P-B3
8	P-K4	QN-Q2
9	R-Q1	N-N3
10	Q-B5	B-N5
11	B-KN5	N-R5
12	Q-R3	NxN
13	PxN	NxP
14	BxP	Q-N3
15	B-B4	NxQBP
16	B-B5	KR-K1ch
17	K-B1	B-K3
18	BxQ	BxBch
19	K-N1	N-K7ch
20	K-B1	NxPch
21	K-N1	N-K7ch
22	K-B1	N-B6ch

Illustration 189

23	K-N1	PxB
24	Q-N4	R-R5
25	QxP	NxR

26	P-KR3	RxP
27	K-R2	NxP
28	R-K1	RxR
29	Q-Q8ch	B-B1
30	NxR	B-Q4
31	N-B3	N-K5
32	Q-N8	P-QN4
33	P-R4	P-R4
34	N-K5	K-N2
35	K-N1	B-B4ch
36	K-B1	N-N6ch
37	K-K1	B-N5ch
38	K-Q1	B-N6ch
39	K-B1	N-K7ch
40	K-N1	N-B6ch
41	K-B1	R-QB7 mate

QUEEN'S GAMBIT DECLINED
Moscow, 1955

PETROSIAN	TAIMANOV
WHITE	BLACK

1	P-Q4	N-KB3
2	P-QB4	P-K3
3	N-KB3	P-Q4
4	N-B3	P-B3
5	P-K3	QN-Q2
6	B-Q3	B-N5
7	0-0	0-0
8	Q-B2	B-Q3
9	P-QN3	PxP

10	PxP	P-K4
11	B-N2	R-K1
12	N-K4	NxN
13	BxN	P-KR3
14	QR-Q1	PxP
15	B-R7ch	K-R1
16	RxP	B-B4
17	R-B4	Q-K2
18	R-K4	Q-B1
19	R-R4	P-B3
20	B-N6	R-K2
21	R-R5	B-Q3
22	R-Q1	B-K4
23	B-R3	P-QB4

Illustration 190

| 24 | N-R4 | Resigns |

SICILIAN DEFENSE
Portoroz, 1958

FISCHER	·	LARSEN
WHITE		BLACK
1	P-K4	P-QB4
2	N-KB3	P-Q3
3	P-Q4	PxP
4	NxP	N-KB3
5	N-QB3	P-KN3
6	B-K3	B-N2
7	P-B3	0-0
8	Q-Q2	N-B3
9	B-QB4	NxN
10	BxN	B-K3
11	B-N3	Q-R4
12	0-0-0	P-QN4
13	K-N1	P-N5
14	N-Q5	BxN
15	BxB	QR-B1
16	B-N3	R-B2
17	P-KR4	Q-QN4
18	P-R5	KR-B1
19	PxP	RPxP
20	P-N4	P-R4
21	P-N5	N-R4
22	RxN	PxR

(See illustration 191)

23	P-N6	P-K4
24	PxPch	K-B1
25	B-K3	P-Q4
26	PxP	RxKBP

Illustration 191

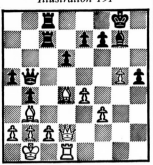

Position after 22 ... PxR

27	P-Q6	R-KB3
28	B-N5	Q-N2
29	BxR	BxB
30	P-Q7	R-Q1
31	Q-R6ch	Resigns

SICILIAN DEFENSE
Bled, 1959

FISCHER	BENKO
WHITE	BLACK
1 P-K4	P-QB4
2 N-KB3	N-QB3
3 P-Q4	PxP
4 NxP	N-B3
5 N-QB3	P-Q3
6 B-QB4	Q-N3
7 KN-K2	P-K3
8 0-0	B-K2
9 B-N3	0-0

10	K-R1	N-QR4
11	B-N5	Q-B4
12	P-B4	P-N4
13	N-N3	P-N5
14	P-K5	PxP
15	BxN	PxB
16	N/B-K4	Q-Q5
17	Q-R5	NxB
18	Q-R6	PxP
19	N-R5	P-B4

Illustration 192

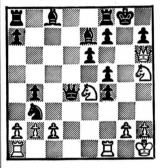

20	QR-Q1	Q-K4
21	N/K-B6ch	BxN
22	NxBch	QxN
23	QxQ	N-B4
24	Q-N5ch	K-R1
25	Q-K7	B-R3
26	QxN	BxR
27	RxB	Resigns

QUEEN'S GAMBIT DECLINED

St. Petersburg, 1909

	RUBINSTEIN	EM. LASKER
	WHITE	BLACK
1	P-Q4	P-Q4
2	N-KB3	N-KB3
3	P-B4	P-K3
4	B-N5	P-B4
5	BPxP	KPxP
6	N-B3	PxP
7	KNxP	N-B3
8	P-K3	B-K2
9	B-N5	B-Q2
10	BxKN	BxB
11	NxP	BxN
12	PxB	Q-N4
13	BxN	BxB
14	N-K3	0-0-0
15	0-0	KR-K1
16	R-B1	RxN
17	RxBch	PxR

(See illustration 193)

18	Q-B1	RxP
19	PxR	R-Q2
20	QxPch	K-Q1
21	R-B4	P-B4
22	Q-B5	Q-K2
23	QxQch	KxQ
24	RxP	R-Q8ch
25	K-B2	R-Q7ch

Illustration 193

Position after 17 ... PxR

26	K-B3	RxQNP
27	R-QR5	R-N2
28	R-R6	K-B1
29	P-K4	R-QB2
30	P-KR4	K-B2
31	P-N4	K-B1
32	K-B4	K-K2
33	P-R5	P-R3
34	K-B5	K-B2
35	P-K5	R-N2
36	R-Q6	K-K2
37	R-R6	K-B2
38	R-Q6	K-B1
39	R-QB6	K-B2
40	P-R3	Resigns

NIMZO-INDIAN DEFENSE
Moscow, 1961

Illustration 194

	BOTVINNIK	TAL
	WHITE	BLACK
1	P-QB4	N-KB3
2	N-QB3	P-K3
3	P-Q4	B-N5
4	P-QR3	BxNch
5	PxB	P-QN3
6	P-B3	B-R3
7	P-K4	P-Q4
8	BPxP	BxB
9	KxB	PxP
10	B-N5	P-KR3
11	Q-R4ch	P-B3
12	B-R4	PxP
13	R-K1	P-KN4
14	B-B2	Q-K2
15	N-K2	P-N4
16	Q-B2	QxP
17	P-R4	NPxP
18	BxP	QN-Q2
19	N-N3	0-0-0
20	NxP	KR-K1
21	K-B2	NxNch
22	PxN	P-B3
23	R-R1	Q-K2
24	RxP	QxP
25	QxQ	RxQ
26	R-R8ch	N-N1

27	B-N3	K-N2
28	R/R-R1	R-QB1
29	R/R-R7ch	K-N3
30	BxN	P-N5
31	B-Q6	PxP
32	B-B5ch	K-N4
33	R-R4	Resigns

RUY LOPEZ
World Match, 1934

	ALEKHINE	BOGOLUBOV
	WHITE	BLACK
1	P-K4	P-K4
2	N-KB3	N-QB3
3	B-N5	P-QR3
4	B-R4	N-B3
5	BxN	QPxB
6	N-B3	B-Q3
7	P-Q3	P-B4
8	P-KR3	B-K3

9	B-K3	P-R3
10	P-QR4	P-B5
11	P-Q4	PxP
12	BxQP	B-QN5
13	0-0	P-B3
14	P-K5	N-Q4
15	N-K4	N-B5
16	B-B5	BxB
17	QxQch	RxQ
18	NxB	P-QN3
19	N-N7	R-Q2
20	N-Q6ch	K-K2
21	N-Q4	B-Q4
22	P-KN3	NxPch
23	K-R2	N-N4
24	P-B4	N-K5
25	N/6-B5ch	K-Q1
26	NxNP	P-B3
27	QR-Q1	K-B1
28	N/Q-B5	PxP
29	PxP	R-N1

30	P-K6	R/QxN
31	NxR	RxN
32	RxB	PxR
33	R-B8ch	K-B2
34	R-B7ch	K-Q3
35	RxR	KxP
36	R-N6ch	K-K4
37	K-N2	P-N4
38	P-R5	P-Q5
39	RxQRP	P-N5
40	K-B3	P-B6
41	PxP	NPxP
42	R-K6ch	KxR
43	KxN	Resigns

Illustration 195

QUEEN'S GAMBIT DECLINED
Zandvoort, 1936

FINE	TARTAKOVER
WHITE	BLACK
1 P-Q4	P-Q4
2 N-KB3	N-KB3
3 P-B4	P-K3
4 N-B3	B-K2
5 P-K3	0-0
6 B-Q3	P-QN3
7 0-0	B-N2
8 P-QN3	P-B4
9 B-N2	N-B3
10 R-B1	R-B1
11 Q-K2	Q-B2

12	BPxP	KPxP
13	N-QN5	Q-N1
14	PxP	PxP
15	BxN	BxB
16	RxP	N-N5
17	RxR	RxR
18	QN-Q4	NxB
19	QxN	Q-Q3

Illustration 196

20	Q-Q2	Q-R6
21	P-R3	P-N3
22	R-N1	B-K2
23	Q-N2	B-R3
24	QxQ	BxQ
25	R-Q1	K-B1
26	N-K1	B-N2
27	N-Q3	P-QR3
28	R-Q2	K-K2
29	R-B2	K-Q3
30	K-B1	R-B2
31	RxR	KxR
32	P-QN4	B-B3

33	K-K2	K-N3
34	N-B2	P-Q5
35	NxB	BxP
36	N-B4	PxP
37	NxB	Resigns

RUY LOPEZ
The Hague, 1948

EUWE	KERES
WHITE	BLACK
1	P-K4	P-K4
2	N-KB3	N-QB3
3	B-N5	P-QR3
4	B-R4	P-Q3
5	P-B3	P-B4
6	PxP	BxP
7	P-Q4	P-K5
8	N-N5	P-Q4
9	P-B3	P-K6
10	P-KB4	B-Q3
11	Q-B3	Q-B3
12	QxPch	N-K2
13	BxNch	PxB
14	0-0	0-0
15	N-Q2	N-N3
16	P-KN3	QR-K1
17	Q-B2	B-Q6
18	R-K1	RxRch
19	QxR	BxP
20	PxB	NxP

21	QN-B3	N-K7ch
22	K-N2	P-R3
23	Q-Q2	Q-B4
24	Q-K3	PxN
25	B-Q2	B-K5

Illustration 197

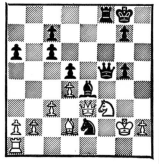

Resigns

DUTCH DEFENSE
Warsaw, 1933

GLUCKSBERG	NAJDORF
WHITE	BLACK
1	P-Q4	P-KB4
2	P-QB4	N-KB3
3	N-QB3	P-K3
4	N-B3	P-Q4
5	P-K3	P-B3
6	B-Q3	B-Q3
7	0-0	0-0
8	N-K2	QN-Q2
9	N-N5	BxPch

10	K-R1	N-N5
11	P-B4	Q-K1
12	P-KN3	Q-R4
13	K-N2	B-N8
14	NxB	Q-R7ch
15	K-B3	P-K4
16	QPxP	QNxPch
17	PxN	NxPch
18	K-B4	N-N3ch

Illustration 198

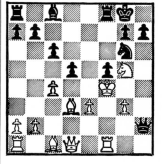

19	K-B3	P-B5
20	KPxP	B-N5ch
21	KxB	N-K4ch
22	PxN	P-R4 mate

KING'S GAMBIT
DECLINED
Match, 1921

EUWE	MAROCZY
WHITE	BLACK
1 P-K4	P-K4
2 P-KB4	B-B4
3 N-KB3	P-Q3
4 P-B3	B-KN5
5 PxP	PxP
6 Q-R4ch	B-Q2
7 Q-B2	Q-K2
8 P-Q4	PxP
9 PxP	B-N5ch
10 N-B3	B-B3
11 B-Q3	BxNch
12 PxB	BxP
13 BxB	P-KB4
14 O-O	PxB

Illustration 199

15 Q-N3	P-B4

16 B-R3	N-KB3
17 BxP	Q-KB2
18 P-B4	P-QN3
19 N-N5	Q-Q2
20 RxN	PxR
21 NxKP	Q-K3
22 R-K1	PxB
23 NxPch	K-B2
24 Q-N7ch	Resigns

QUEEN'S GAMBIT
DECLINED
Hastings, 1934–35

EUWE	THOMAS
WHITE	BLACK
1 P-QB4	P-K3
2 N-QB3	P-Q4
3 P-Q4	N-KB3
4 B-N5	B-K2
5 P-K3	O-O
6 N-B3	QN-Q2
7 R-B1	P-B3
8 B-Q3	PxP
9 BxP	N-Q4
10 BxB	QxB
11 O-O	NxN
12 RxN	P-K4
13 NxP	NxN
14 PxN	QxP
15 P-B4	Q-K2
16 P-B5	P-QN4

17	B-N3	P-N5

Illustration 200

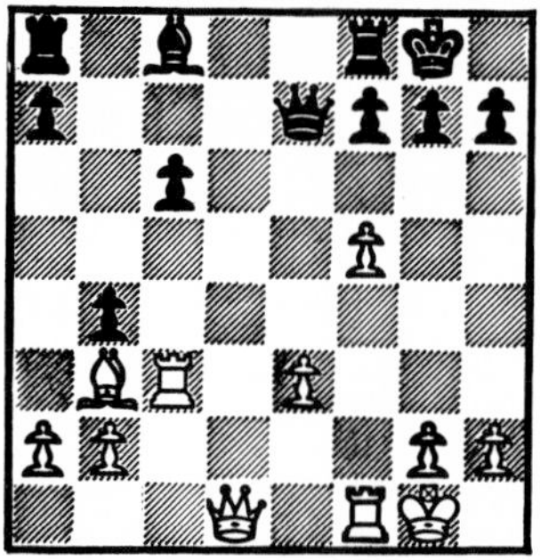

18	P-B6	PxP
19	QRxP	QxPch
20	K-R1	B-N2
21	QRxP	Q-K5
22	Q-Q2	K-R1
23	BxP	QR-B1
24	R/6-B2	QR-Q1
25	Q-N5	R-Q3
26	B-Q5	Resigns

Quiz Solutions

Replies to Recheck Quiz (page 59).

1. Illustration 47 displays the grand range of checks. The Rook can move horizontally and vertically and checks by 1 R–K3 or 1 R–R7. The Bishop, moving on the diagonal, can check by 1 B–B6. The Knight on the far left can check by 1 N–B8 or 1 N–B6; the other Knight by 1 N–B6 or 1 N–B5. And the Pawn can advance, 1 P–Q6, giving check. The total is eight ways to check.

2. In illustration 48, there are four possible interpositions: 1 B–K2, 1 B–K5, 1 R–K2, and 1 N–K5. There are two captures: 1 QxR and 1 BxR. And the King has three possible moves "out of check," 1 K–Q1, 1 K–Q2, and 1 K–B2. There are nine different ways of getting out of check.

3. In illustration 49, White's play is illegal, exposing his King to the line of fire of Black's Rook. Not for a single move may a King be exposed to check. If White believed that his delivery of checkmate superseded all other matters, he was wrong. In theory, White's Queen moves to check Black's King; but, the moment it moves, Black's Rook captures White's King—before White's Queen can move again to capture Black's King. In fact and in law, White's King simply must not be exposed.

If such a move as 1 Q–N8ch were made, it would be ruled illegal, the Queen returned to its prior position, and, per the "touch-move" rule, the Queen would then have to be moved legally. (White has but two legal moves: the futile 1 Q–B5, which allows the Queen to be captured for no recompense, and 1 QxR, which at least gains a Rook for the Queen, and, incidentally, an ending—after 1 ... QxQch and 2 R–N5 or 2 K–R4—which gives Black what is usually a decisive advantage of Queen against Rook but which offers no easy win for Black in these particular circumstances!)

Replies to Summary Quiz (page 60).

1. Any one of White's eight Pawns and either of White's two Knights.
2. White has the choice of 20 moves on his first turn: 16 different Pawn moves and four different Knight moves.
3. 20 replies.
4. The Queen.

5. There is no such piece in orthodox chess.

6. Same answer as in 5.

7. (1) *Capturing* the attacking piece; (2) *moving* out of the line of fire of the attacking piece; and (3) *interposing* a friendly piece on the line of fire between the target King and the attacking piece.

8. The game is over since the King is checkmated or mated.

9. The Knight and the Pawn.

10. The player must retract the illegal move and make a legal one in its place, cognizant of the "touch-move" rule; i.e. he must move his King elsewhere if possible.

11. The move is illegal and must be retracted, substituting a legal one in its place. But here, too, the player is not absolved from the "touch-move" rule.

12. Same as above in case of illegal move.

13. He must capture it if he can.

14. The Pawn must be promoted to a piece of its own color, barring another King.

15. As many as he may be able to promote, plus his original one. Theoretically, he may have nine.

16. Castling is the movement of King and Rook, simultaneously, under the five given conditions (page 34).

17. The Rook. It commands black and white squares, whereas the Bishop commands only black *or* white.

18. Eight.

Solutions to Tactical Checkmates (page 119).

1. 1 QxN! PxQ; 2 R–N1ch, Q–N5; 3 RxQch and mate next.
2. 1 Q–Q3ch! and mate next.
3. 1 BxNch, and 1 ... PxB; 2 N–B6 and mate next, or 1 ... K–N1; 2 N–B6ch and mate next.
4. 1 B–B8 dis. ch, B–R4; 2 QxBch and mate next.
5. 1 Q–R6 and mate next.
6. 1 R–R5 and mate next or after 1 ... N–K7ch; 2 BxN, Q–Q8ch; 3 BxQ.
7. 1 N–B6ch, K–R1 (or 1 ... K–N2; 2 N–R5 dbl. ch and mate next); 2 N–N4 dis. ch, NxQ; 3 B–B6ch and mate next.
8. 1 QxP and mate follows.
9. 1 N–N6ch, and 1 ... K–N1; 2 Q–N7ch and mate next, or 1 ... QxN; 2 Q–B8ch, Q–N1; 3 BxPch and mate next.
10. 1 QxBch, K–K5; 2 B–Q3ch and mate next.
11. 1 QxPch, QxQ; 2 N/N–B7ch and mate next.
12. 1 Q–R7ch, K–B1; 2 Q–R8ch, K–K2; 3 N–B5ch and mate next.

Solutions for Exercises in Tactics (page 121).

1. 1 B–Q3ch, P–N3; 2 R–R8ch, KxR; 3 Q–B8ch, K–R2; 4 QxBPch, K–R1; 5 Q–B8ch, K–R2; 6 BxPch, KxB; 7 Q–N8 mate.
2. 1 N–B7ch, K–R2; 2 QxPch, PxQ; 3 N–N5 dis. ch, K–R1; 4 R–R7 mate.
3. 1 R–KR5, QxR (else, 2 RxQ or RxR); 2 QxPch, PxQ; 3 BxP mate.

4. 1 BxP, QxQ; 2 RxNP, and White wins.

5. 1 RxB, PxR; 2 N–B6ch, PxN; 3 Q–R6.

6. 1 RxPch, KxR; 2 Q–R3ch, K–N2; 3 B–R6ch, and mate next.

7. 1 R–KR5ch, PxR; 2 N–B5 mate.

8. 1 NxKBP, KxN; 2 QxPch, K–N3; 3 Q–B5 mate or 1 . . . Q–K2; 2 NxR, and Black wins.

9. 1 Q–KR8ch! KxQ; 2 P–N7ch, K–N1; 3 B–R7ch! KxB or K–B2; 4 P–N8(Q) mate.

10. 1 NxP wins the Pawn since 1 . . . BxQ; 2 BxPch, K–K2; 3 N–Q5 is mate.

11. 1 RxN, QxR; 2 R–Q8! QxR (else, 3 R–R8 mate); 3 NxPch etc.

12. 1 QxPch, QxQ; 2 RxQch, KxR; 3 R–R1ch etc.

13. 1 . . . RxP; 2 R/2xR, RxR; 3 RxR, Q–R8ch etc.

14. 1 . . . RxR; 2 QxR, Q–Q3! etc.

15. 1 . . . N–B6ch; 2 PxN, Q–B8ch; 3 KxQ, B–R6ch; 4 K–N1, R–K8 mate.

16. 1 . . . RxPch; 2 PxR, Q–N8ch; 3 K–R4, P–N4ch etc.

17. 1 . . . B–R3!; 2 R–K1 (or 2 BxB? Q–B7ch and Black mates in 2 moves), BxBch; 3 QxB, R–B8ch etc.

18. 1 . . . N–K7ch; 2 RxN, Q–R8ch, etc.

19. 1 . . . QxRch; 2 BxQ, N–B6 mate.

20. 1 . . . N–N6ch; 2 PxN, Q–R6ch; 3 K–N1, BxBch and mate next.

21. 1 . . . R–Q7; 2 BxR (else, 2 . . . Q–R8 mate), N–Q5! etc.

22. 1 . . . Q–N6; 2 BxR (else, 2 . . . QxNP mate), P–B6! etc.

23. 1 . . . R–R1; 2 QxR, N–R2! and Black soon mates.

24. 1 . . . RxPch; 2 KxR, Q–K7ch; 3 K–R1, R–Q7 etc. or 3 R–B2, R–N1ch etc.